Baby Girl Names:
What other parents are choosing

Almost 6,000 names for your baby girl

James and Rose Hughes

CONTENTS

Choosing your baby's name

Congratulations! With a baby on the way you are celebrating your good news, letting others know and starting to think practically about the 1001 things that you need for a brand new tiny person.

And top of that list – is a name.

After all, it is going to stay with them for life and even shape people's perceptions of them for years to come.

So this book contains almost 6,000 names chosen by other parents over the last year – arranged alphabetically. We have also included the top 101 names so you can see exactly what is popular right now.

When we were expecting our first child we did our best to keep the name choosing process a secret. Not because we didn't appreciate our families' input (even if there can sometimes be an awful lot of it...). But because it was such an important and personal decision that we wanted to make the choice between us, without feeling that we had to satisfy anyone else.

After all – we'd done that over the wedding and didn't want to go there again.

Sometimes it will feel that *everyone* has an opinion. Right down to the spelling.

What you do about that is up to you. Some welcome the infinite wisdom of relatives/the chap you sat next to on the bus. Others just wish everyone would keep their nose out.

We decided to go for total lockdown on the name. Hiding

the books and The List whenever one of our mothers called round for a chat.

In fact, we went one stage further and drew up a fake list to leave lying around, containing some of the worst names that we had stumbled across. I know. We're really bad.

One of the things we noticed (when we weren't being mean to our mums…) is that none of the real names we found trawling the books felt, well, very *now*.

Some felt like they had been copied from edition to edition for many, many years and authors had made no attempt to update them.

So this book is different. It gives you a selection of the most up to date names that other parents are using – and choosing to call their babies now.

That doesn't mean that they are all well-known names – far from it. There are many that we had never heard of before. But they have all been registered by parents applying for a birth certificate over the last couple of years.

And that is what makes this book different. They are all names that have actually been used by other parents, who have gone through what you are going through now.

They have thought about it, worried about it, lost sleep about it, consulted about it, fallen out with their other half about it… and eventually chosen the name they want for their child.

So, what follows is the end result of millions of parents' time and effort – presented to help you.

Some are vintage, some are modern. Some are drawn from

other parts of the word or from literature. Some will make you shake your head and roll your eyes – and others will have you reaching for your pad of names to scribble them down.

But above all they should make you think. About how the names sound, how they look, how they're spelt and how they fit with the baby's surname.

We've included the latest trends from celebrities and the most popular girls' names according to data collected by officials.

One huge trend right now is unusual spellings. This marries a traditional sounding name with a little bit of individualism – a chance to stand out. So, as far as possible, we have included as many different spellings as we have been able to find in the records.

For example, the name "Zara". Not that traditional to start with, it has been recreated by parents keen to put their own spin on the name.

This book includes variations such as Zaara, Zaarah, Zarah, Zerah and Xara to pick just a few. Parents increasingly want to find names that don't just sound beautiful – but look beautiful too.

So, grab a pad, a pen and a drink and start your journey to picking the perfect name.

What are other parents choosing?

It only seems a few years ago parents were picking, well, unusual names. That seems to have been driven by a spate of celebrities coming up with, frankly, fairly weird choices.

We all remember Apple – but there was also Audio, Blue Ivy and Cosimo.

If they were on your list, then sincere apologies. I'm sure your child will still grow up just fine…

But there seems to have been a big swing against these sorts of "out there" names in the popularity stakes.

There hasn't, for example, been a huge rush of parents desperate to copy their favourite stars and christen their children Cricket or Birdie.

Instead the top ten most popular names list has been surprisingly static over the last few years. And it has been dominated by familiar, well-known and, perhaps, comfortable sounding names.

See what you think…

1. Amelia
2. Olivia
3. Emily
4. Isla
5. Ava
6. Ella
7. Jessica
8. Isabella
9. Eva
10. Poppy

Amelia, Olivia and Isla have happily stuck around in the top ten for many years now. Ella and Mia are the only new entries, moving up from just outside the top ten.

Other names further down the list wax and wane in popularity, according to taste, fashion and even films. For example, we are bracing for a glut of *Star Wars* named babies (no sign of us being overrun by Reys at the moment but, in a galaxy far, far away...)

Don't panic!

Choosing a name is a big responsibility. But it's nothing compared to having to care for a child for the best part of the next two decades (oh, who are kidding? The rest of their lives...).

It may seem overwhelming trying to find the perfect name but, here's the really big secret about baby naming: whichever one you pick will turn out to be perfect.

Partly because of the time, attention, research and love you will pour into it. But also because your baby will grow to fit the name and come to embody it in your mind and the minds of your family.

In years to come you will look at her, shake your head and wonder: 'How did we ever even consider calling her something else?'

So, we haven't included any meanings or origins of names in our book. Not least because it felt like every single one we looked up seemed to be a variation on "noble."

This is about starting the thought process – not complicating it further for you.

So, enjoy the process. Try things out. Play with spellings. Laugh at what other parents choose to do. But, most of all, have fun doing it.

Oh, and good luck with the baby!

James and Rose

101 Most Popular Girls' Names

1. Amelia	35. Layla	69. Penelope
2. Olivia	36. Rosie	70. Anna
3. Emily	37. Maya	71. Nancy
4. Isla	38. Esme	72. Zara
5. Ava	39. Elizabeth	73. Maria
6. Ella	40. Lola	74. Darcie
7. Jessica	41. Willow	75. Maryam
8. Isabella	42. Ivy	76. Megan
9. Mia	43. Erin	77. Darcey
10. Poppy	44. Holly	78. Lottie
11. Sophie	45. Emilia	79. Mila
12. Sophia	46. Molly	80. Heidi
13. Lily	47. Ellie	81. Lexi
14. Grace	48. Jasmine	82. Lacey
15. Evie	49. Eliza	83. Francesca
16. Scarlett	50. Lilly	84. Robyn
17. Ruby	51. Abigail	85. Bethany
18. Chloe	52. Georgia	86. Julia
19. Isabelle	53. Maisie	87. Sara
20. Daisy	54. Eleanor	88. Aisha
21. Freya	55. Hannah	89. Darcy
22. Phoebe	56. Harriet	90. Zoe
23. Florence	57. Amber	91. Clara
24. Alice	58. Bella	92. Victoria
25. Charlotte	59. Thea	93. Beatrice
26. Sienna	60. Annabelle	94. Hollie
27. Matilda	61. Emma	95. Arabella
28. Evelyn	62. Amelie	96. Sarah
29. Eva	63. Harper	97. Maddison
30. Millie	64. Gracie	98. Leah
31. Sofia	65. Rose	99. Katie
32. Lucy	66. Summer	100. Aria
33. Elsie	67. Martha	101. Eloise
34. Imogen	68. Violet	

1
NAMES BEGINNING WITH A

Aabidah
Aabish
Aadhya
Aadya
Aaeesha
Aafia
Aafiya
Aafiyah
Aafreen
Aahana
Aahna
Aaila
Aaima
Aaira
Aairah
Aaisha
Aaishah
Aaiza
Aaizah
Aakifa
Aakifah
Aala
Aalayah

Aaleyah
Aalia
Aalimah
Aaliya
Aaliyah
Aaliyah-Mai
Aaliyah-May
Aaliyah-Rose
Aamal
Aamanee
Aamaya
Aamena
Aamenah
Aamilah
Aamina
Aaminah
Aamira
Aamirah
Aamna
Aanaya
Aanika
Aaniya
Aaniyah

Aanya
Aara
Aaradhya
Aarathana
Aaria
Aariah
Aariana
Aarifa
Aarifah
Aarika
Aariya
Aariyah
Aarna
Aarohi
Aarushi
Aarvi
Aarya
Aaryana
Aarzoo
Aashi
Aashna
Aashvi
Aasia

Aasiya	Abrielle	Adelyn
Aasiyah	Abrish	Adelynn
Aastha	Abyan	Aden
Aatikah	Abygail	Adeola
Aava	Acacia	Aderyn
Aavya	Ada	Adesewa
Aaya	Adaeze	Adesuwa
Aayah	Adah	Adhya
Aayana	Adalia	Adi
Aayat	Adalie	Adiba
Aayla	Adalind	Adina
Aayliah	Adaline	Aditi
Aayrah	Adalyn	Aditri
Aazeen	Adalynn	Adna
Abbey	Adama	Adora
Abbi	Ada-May	Adriana
Abbie	Adan	Adrianna
Abbie-Mae	Adana	Adrianne
Abbie-Rose	Adanna	Adriel
Abbigail	Adara	Adrielle
Abby	Ada-Rose	Adrija
Abeeha	Addiena	Adrina
Abeer	Addilyn	Adwoa
Abeera	Addison	Aela
Abeerah	Addyson	Aella
Abena	Adea	Aemilia
Abi	Adebola	Aerin
Abia	Adeeba	Aeris
Abida	Adeela	Aerith
Abigail	Adeena	Aeryn
Abigail-Rose	Adeeva	Aeva
Abigayle	Adel	Afeefah
Abigel	Adela	Afia
Abiha	Adelaide	Afifa
Abira	Adele	Afifah
Abisha	Adelia	Afiya
Abrar	Adelina	Afiyah
Abrianna	Adeline	Afizah
Abriella	Adelle	Afnaan

Afnan
Afra
Afrah
Afreen
Afrida
Afsa
Afsah
Afsana
Afseen
Afsheen
Agamjot
Agata
Agatha
Agne
Agnes
Agnieszka
Agota
Ahana
Ahlaam
Ahlam
Aibhlinn
Aicha
Aida
Aidel
Aidy
Aiesha
Aikaterini
Aiko
Aila
Ailah
Ailbhe
Aileen
Ailish
Ailla
Ailsa
Aima
Aiman
Aimee
Aimee-Lee

Aimee-Leigh
Aimee-Rose
Aimen
Aimie
Aina
Aine
Ainhoa
Ainsley
Aira
Airah
Aisha
A'isha
Aishah
Aishani
Aishat
Aishleen
Aishwarya
Aisla
Aislin
Aisling
Aislinn
Aissata
Aissatou
Aiste
Aitana
Aiva
Aivah
Aiya
Aiyana
Aiyanna
Aiyat
Aiyla
Aiylah
Aiysha
Aiyzah
Aiza
Aizah
Ajla
Ajooni

Ajuni
Ajwa
Akasha
Akeelah
Aki
Akifah
Akilah
Akira
Akirah
Akosua
Akshara
Aksharaa
Akshata
Akshaya
Akshayah
Akshita
Akvile
Ala
Alaa
Alabama
Alaia
Alaia-Mai
Alaina
Alaiya
Alaiyah
Alaiza
Alana
Alanah
Alana-Mae
Alana-Rose
Alani
Alanis
Alanna
Alannah
Alannah-Mae
Alanta
Alantis
Alanya
Alara

Alarna
Alarnie
Alaska
Alaura
Alaw
Alaya
Alayah
Alayah-Rose
Alayla
Alayna
Alaynah
Alaysia
Alba
Albany
Alba-Rose
Alberta
Albina
Alea
Aleah
Aleasha
Alecia
Aleeah
Aleema
Aleemah
Aleen
Aleena
Aleenah
Aleesa
Aleesha
Aleeya
Aleeza
Aleezah
Aleezay
Alegra
Aleia
Aleigha
Aleisha
Alejandra
Aleksa

Aleksandra
Alena
Alero
Alesha
Alesia
Alessa
Alessandra
Alessia
Alethea
Aletheia
Aletta
Alex
Alexa
Alexa-Mae
Alexandra
Alexandria
Alexandrina
Alexa-Rose
Alexcia
Alexi
Alexia
Alexia-Mae
Alexie
Alexis
Alexis-Mae
Alexis-Rose
Alexus
Alexys
Aleya
Aleyah
Aleyna
Ali
Alia
Aliah
Aliana
Alianna
Alica
Alice
Alice-Jane

Alice-Mae
Alice-Marie
Alice-May
Alice-Rose
Alicia
Alicja
Aliki
Alima
Alimah
Alin
Alina
Alinah
Aliona
Alis
Alisa
Alise
Alisha
Alishah
Alisha-May
Alishba
Alishbah
Alisia
Alison
Alissa
Alisse
Alissia
Alivia
Alivia-Rose
Alix
Aliya
Aliyah
Aliyyah
Aliz
Aliza
Alizah
Alizay
Alize
Aljawharah
Allana

Allanah
Alle
Allegra
Alleyah
Allie
Allison
Alliyah
Ally
Alma
Almas
Almina
Almira
Alora
Alreem
Althea
Aluna
Alva
Alvina
Alya
Alyana
Alyanna
Alyce
Alycia
Alys
Alysa
Alysha
Alysia
Alyssa
Alyssa-Mae
Alyssa-Rose
Alyssia
Alyssia-Mae
Alyvia
Alyza
Alyzah
Amaal
Amaanah
Amaani
Amaara

Amaarah
Amaaya
Amaia
Amaima
Amaira
Amairah
Amaiya
Amaiyah
Amal
Amala
Amalee
Amali
Amalia
Amalie
Aman
Amana
Amanah
Amanat
Amanda
Amandeep
Amani
Amanpreet
Amar
Amara
Amarachi
Amarachukwu
Amarah
Amara-Rose
Amari
Amariah
Amaris
Amarisa
Amarissa
Amariyah
Amarpreet
Amaryllis
Amatullah
Amaya
Amayah

Amaya-Rae
Amaya-Rose
Amayra
Amba
Ambar
Amber
Amber-Grace
Amberley
Amber-Louise
Amberly
Amber-May
Amber-Rose
Ambika
Ambra
Amedeea
Ameelah
Ameena
Ameenah
Ameera
Ameerah
Ameila
Ameilia
Ameira
Amel
Amela
Amelia
Amelia-
Amelia-Faith
Amelia-Faye
Amelia-Grace
Ameliah
Amelia-Jade
Amelia-Jane
Amelia-Jayne
Amelia-Jean
Amelia-Leigh
Amelia-Lillie
Amelia-Lilly
Amelia-Lily

Amelia-Louise
Amelia-Mae
Amelia-Mai
Amelia-Marie
Amelia-May
Amelia-Rae
Amelia-Rose
Amelie
Amelie-Mae
Amelie-Rose
Amelija
Ameliya
Ameliyah
Amelja
Amelle
Amellia
Amelya
Amen
Amena
Amera
Amerie
Amethyst
Ameya
Ami
Amia
Amiah
Amie
Amiee
Amiera
Amiira
Amika
Amila
Amilah
Amilee
Amilia
Amilie
Amima
Amina
Aminah

Aminata
Amine
Amira
Amirah
Amisha
Amita
Amity
Amiya
Amiyah
Amiyah-Rose
Ammaarah
Ammara
Ammarah
Amna
Amnah
Amour
Amra
Amreece
Amreen
Amreet
Amrit
Amrita
Amy
Amya
Amyah
Amy-Grace
Amyleigh
Amy-Leigh
Amylia
Amy-Louise
Amyra
Amyrah
Amy-Rose
An
Ana
Anaaya
Anaayah
Anabel
Anabela

Anabell
Anabella
Anabelle
Anabeth
Anabia
Anabiya
Anae
Anaelle
Anagha
Anah
Anahita
Anaia
Anaiah
Anais
Anaisha
Anais-Rose
Anaiya
Anaiyah
Analeigh
Analise
Ana-Lucia
Anam
Anamaria
Ana-Maria
Anamika
Anamta
Anannya
Ananya
Ananyaa
Anara
Anashe
Anastacia
Anastasia
Anastasija
Anastazia
Anastazja
Anaum
Anaya
Anayah

Anays	Angie	Anna-Leigh
Anca	Ani	Annalie
Andi	Ania	Annaliese
Andia	Aniah	Annalisa
Andie	Aniela	Annalise
Andra	Anika	Annalyse
Andrada	Anila	Annam
Andrea	Anina	Anna-Mae
Andreea	Aniqa	Anna-Maria
Andreia	Anisa	Anna-Rose
Andreja	Anisah	Anna-Sophia
Andria	Anise	Annaya
Andriana	Anisha	Annayah
Andzelika	Anishka	Anne
Aneeka	Anisia	Anneka
Aneeqa	Anissa	Annelie
Aneesa	Anita	Anneliese
Aneesah	Aniya	Annelise
Aneesha	Aniyah	Anne-Marie
Aneira	Aniyah-Rose	Annest
Anesa	Anja	Annette
Anest	Anjali	Anni
Anesu	Anjana	Annie
Aneta	Anjika	Annie-Mae
Anetta	Anjola	Annie-Mai
Aneya	Anjolaoluwa	Annie-May
Anfal	Ann	Annie-Rae
Angel	Anna	Annie-Rose
Angela	Annabel	Annika
Angelene	Annabell	Annis
Angelica	Annabella	Anniyah
Angelie	Annabelle	Annmaria
Angelika	Annabelle-Rose	Annmarie
Angelina	Annabel-Rose	Ann-Marie
Angeline	Annabeth	Annora
Angelique	Annah	Annya
Angel-May	Annalea	Anokhi
Angel-Rose	Annalee	Anouk
Angharad	Annaleigh	Anoushka

Anouska
Anshika
Anthea
Antigone
Antoinette
Antonella
Antonia
Antonia-Maria
Antonina
Anum
Anuoluwa
Anureet
Anusha
Anushka
Anvi
Anvika
Anvita
Anwen
Anya
Anyah
Anya-Rose
Anzal
Aoibhe
Aoibheann
Aoibhinn
Aoife
Aoife-Belle
Aparna
Aphra
Apolline
Apolonia
Apphia
April
April-Rose
Apryl
Aqsa
Aqsah
Ara
Arabel

Arabella
Arabella-Grace
Arabella-Rose
Arabelle
Aradhana
Aradhya
Araiya
Araminta
Araya
Arayah
Areeba
Areebah
Areej
Areen
Areesa
Areesha
Aresha
Areya
Arfa
Ari
Aria
Ariadna
Ariadne
Ariah
Arial
Ariam
Aria-Mae
Ariana
Arianah
Ariane
Arianna
Arianna-Rose
Arianne
Arianwen
Ariarna
Aria-Rose
Ariba
Aribah
Aribella

Ariel
Ariela
Ariele
Ariella
Arielle
Arienna
Arienne
Arietta
Arifa
Arifah
Arij
Arija
Arin
Arina
Ariona
Arisa
Arisha
Arissa
Ariya
Ariyah
Ariyah-Rose
Ariyana
Arizona
Arjin
Arla
Arla-Rose
Arlene
Arleya
Arlia
Arlie
Arlo
Armaani
Armani
Armela
Armina
Arna
Arnica
Arnika
Arohi

Arooj	Ashleigh-Rose	Atiyah
Aroosa	Ashley	Atlanta
Aroosh	Ashlie	Atlantis
Aroush	Ashling	Attica
Arrabella	Ashlyn	Aubree
Arriella	Ashlynn	Aubrey
Arrietty	Ashmeet	Aubrey-Rose
Arsema	Ashmita	Aubrie
Arshi	Ashna	Auden
Arshia	Ashton	Audra
Arshiya	Asia	Audrey
Artemis	Asiya	August
Arusha	Asiyah	Augusta
Arushi	Asli	Auguste
Arwa	Asma	Aukse
Arwaa	Asmaa	Aura
Arwen	Asmah	Auraya
Arya	Asmara	Aureja
Aryahi	Asmin	Aurelia
Aryam	Aspen	Aurelie
Aryana	Asra	Aurelija
Aryanna	Asta	Auri
Aryia	Aster	Aurianna
Arzu	Astera	Aurora
Asal	Astra	Aurora-Mae
Aseel	Astrid	Aurora-Rose
Asees	Asya	Austeja
Asenath	Atalya	Autumn
Asfiya	Atara	Autumn-Lily
Asha	Atarah	Autumn-Rose
Ashalina	Atena	Ava
Ashanti	Atene	Ava-
Asher	Athalie	Avaani
Ashika	Athea	Ava-Belle
Ashira	Athena	Ava-Grace
Ashlea	Athina	Avah
Ashlee	Atika	Avaiya
Ashleen	Atinuke	Ava-Jade
Ashleigh	Atiya	Ava-Jane

Ava-Jayne
Avalee
Avaleigh
Ava-Leigh
Ava-Lillie
Ava-Lilly
Ava-Lily
Avalon
Ava-Louise
Avalyn
Ava-Mae
Ava-Mai
Ava-Marie
Ava-May
Avana
Avangeline
Avani
Avannah
Avantika
Ava-Rae
Ava-Rai
Avarni
Ava-Rose
Avaya
Avayah
Aveen
Aveline
Avelyn
Averie
Avery
Avia
Aviah
Aviana
Avianna
Avie
Avika
Avina
Avital
Avleen

Avneet
Avni
Avnoor
Avreet
Avril
Awa
Awel
Awen
Awin
Axelle
Aya
Ayaan
Ayaana
Ayaanah
Ayaat
Ayah
Ayala
Ayan
Ayana
Ayanah
Ayane
Ayanna
Ayat
Ayca
Ayda
Ayda-Rose
Ayelet
Ayesha
Ayeshah
Ayeza
Ayisha
Ayla
Ayla-Grace
Aylah
Ayla-Jade
Ayla-Mae
Ayla-Mai
Ayla-May
Ayla-Rose

Ayleen
Aylin
Ayline
Ayman
Aymen
Aymira
Ayna
Ayomide
Ayomikun
Ayra
Ayrah
Ayse
Aysegul
Aysel
Aysha
Ayshah
Aysu
Ayushi
Ayva
Ayvah
Ayza
Ayzah
Azaelia
Azalea
Azalia
Azaliah
Azara
Azaria
Azariah
Azeen
Azima
Aziza
Azka
Azma
Azra
Azrah
Azura
Azzurra

2
NAMES BEGINNING WITH B

Baani
Baby
Bahar
Baila
Bailee
Bailey
Bailey-May
Bailey-Rae
Bailie
Bakhtawar
Balqees
Balqis
Bana
Baneen
Baneet
Bani
Bao
Barbara
Barbora
Bareera
Bareerah
Barin
Barirah
Barley
Basma
Batool
Batsheva
Batya
Bay
Bayan
Baye
Bayla

Baylee
Bayleigh
Baylie
Bea
Beata
Beatrice
Beatris
Beatrix
Beatriz
Beau
Beaux
Bebe
Beca
Becca
Bee
Bejna
Bela
Belinda
Bella
Bella-Ann
Bella-Grace
Bella-Louise
Bella-Mae
Bella-Mai
Bella-Maria
Bella-Marie
Bella-May
Bella-Rae
Bellarose
Bella-Rose
Bellatrix
Belle

Benedetta
Benedicte
Benita
Beren
Berenice
Berenika
Berfin
Bernadette
Bernice
Berra
Berrie
Berry
Berta
Bertha
Beryl
Bess
Bessie
Beth
Bethan
Bethanie
Bethannie
Bethany
Bethany-Rose
Bethel
Bethia
Bethlehem
Betsan
Betsey
Betsi
Betsie
Betsy
Betsy-Blu

Betsy-Rae
Betsy-Rose
Bette
Bettie
Bettina
Bettsy
Betty
Betul
Beulah
Beverly
Bexley
Beyla
Beyza
Bhadra
Bhavika
Bhavneet
Bhavya
Bianca
Bianka
Bibi
Bilan
Billi
Billie
Billie-Jean
Billie-Jo
Billie-Mae
Billie-Mai
Billie-May
Billie-Rae
Billie-Rose
Billy
Bilqis
Binky
Binta
Bintou
Birdie
Birrah
Bisma
Bismah

Blair
Blaire
Blaise
Blake
Blanca
Blanka
Blen
Blessing
Blimi
Bliss
Blossom
Blousie
Blu
Blue
Bluebell
Bluebelle
Blythe
Bo
Bobbi
Bobbie
Bobbie-Jo
Bobbie-Leigh
Bobbie-Rose
Bobbi-Jo
Bobbi-Lou
Bobby
Bodhi
Boe
Boglarka
Boluwatife
Bonita
Bonni
Bonnie
Bonnie-Leigh
Bonnie-Lou
Bonnie-Mae
Bonnie-Marie
Bonnie-May
Bonnie-Rae

Bonnie-Rose
Bonny
Bora
Bouchra
Boux
Bow
Bowe
Bozhidara
Bracha
Brae
Branwen
Brea
Breanna
Bree
Breeze
Brenna
Bria
Briana
Brianna
Brianna-Leigh
Brianne
Briar
Briar-Rose
Bridey
Bridget
Bridie
Brieanna
Briella
Brielle
Brienne
Brigitte
Brinley
Briony
Britney
Brittany
Brodie
Brody
Brogan
Bronagh

Bronte
Bronwen
Bronwyn
Brook
Brooke
Brookelyn
Brooke-Rose
Brooklyn
Brooklynn
Brooklyn-Rose
Brucha
Bruna
Brydie
Bryher
Bryna
Bryonie
Bryony
Buse
Bushra

3
NAMES BEGINNING WITH C

Cadence
Cadi
Cadie
Caelyn
Caia
Cailyn
Caira
Caitlin
Caitlyn
Caleigh
Cali
Calia
Calise
Calista
Calla
Calleigh
Calli
Callie
Callie-Mae
Callie-Mai
Callie-May
Callie-Rose
Calliope
Cally
Camelia
Camellia
Cameron
Cami
Camila
Cami-Leigh
Cami-Li
Camilla

Camille
Cammie
Candice
Candy
Cansu
Caoilainn
Caoimhe
Capri
Caprice
Cara
Caragh
Carah
Carey
Cari
Cariad
Carin
Carina
Caris
Carissa
Carla
Carlee
Carley
Carlie
Carlota
Carlotta
Carly
Carmel
Carmela
Carmella
Carmen
Carol
Carolina

Caroline
Carolyn
Carrie
Carys
Casey
Casey-Leigh
Casey-Mai
Casey-May
Casi
Casiana
Cassandra
Cassia
Cassidy
Cassidy-Rose
Cassie
Cassiopeia
Cataleya
Catalina
Catarina
Catelyn
Caterina
Catherina
Catherine
Cathleen
Cathryn
Catrin
Catrina
Catriona
Cattleya
Caydence
Cayla
Caysie

Ceanna
Cece
Cecelia
Cecile
Cecilia
Cecily
Cecylia
Ceinwen
Celeste
Celestine
Celia
Celina
Celine
Celyn
Cemre
Ceren
Ceridwen
Ceryn
Cerys
Ceyda
Chaise
Chana
Chanae
Chanai
Chandni
Chanel
Chanelle
Chani
Chantelle
Chardonnay
Charis
Charissa
Charity
Charlea
Charlee
Charleigh
Charlene
Charley
Charley-Mae

Charley-Rose
Charli
Charlie
Charlie-Anne
Charlie-Mai
Charlie-Rae
Charlie-Rose
Charlize
Charlotte
Charlotte-Ann
Charlotte-Louise
Charlotte-May
Charlotte-Rose
Charly
Charlyn
Charmaine
Charmi
Charvi
Chase
Chava
Chavi
Chaya
Che
Chelsea
Chelsea-Leigh
Chelsey
Chelsie
Chen
Chenai
Cher
Cherie
Cherish
Cherrie
Cherry
Cheryl
Cheyanne
Cheyenne
Chiamaka
Chiara

Chidera
Chidinma
Chikamso
Chimamanda
Chinaza
Chinenye
Chioma
Chisom
Chizara
Chizaram
Chizitere
Chloe
Chloe-Ann
Chloe-Anne
Chloe-Lee
Chloe-Louise
Chloe-Mae
Chloe-Marie
Chloe-May
Chloe-Rae
Chloe-Rose
Chrissy
Christa
Christabel
Christal
Christiana
Christie
Christina
Christine
Christy
Chyna
Chyna-Rose
Ciana
Cianna
Ciara
Ciarah
Cicely
Cici
Cienna

Cindy
Claire
Clancy
Clara
Clarabelle
Clara-Rose
Clare
Clarice
Clarissa
Clarke
Claudia
Clea
Clemence
Clemency
Clementina
Clementine
Cleo
Cleopatra
Clio
Clodagh
Cloe
Clover
Cobie
Coco
Codi
Codie
Cody
Colette
Comfort
Connie
Connie-Leigh
Connie-Louise
Connie-Mae
Connie-Rae
Connie-Rose
Constance
Constantina
Constanza
Consuela

Cooper
Cora
Corah
Coral
Coralie
Coraline
Cora-Rae
Cordelia
Corinna
Corinne
Cornelia
Cosima
Courtney
Courtney-Rose
Cressida
Crina
Cristiana
Cristina
Crystal
Crystal-Rose
Csenge
Cydney
Cynthia
Cyra

4
NAMES BEGINNING WITH D

Daania
Daanya
Daenerys
Dafne
Dahlia
Daiana
Daisey
Daisie
Daisie-Mae
Daisy
Daisy-Ann
Daisy-Anne
Daisy-Belle
Daisy-Grace
Daisy-Jane
Daisy-Lee
Daisy-Leigh
Daisy-Lou
Daisy-Louise
Daisy-Mae
Daisy-Mai
Daisy-Marie
Daisy-May
Daisy-Rae
Daisy-Rose
Daizy
Dakota
Daksha
Dalal
Dalia
Dallas
Damaris
Damilola
Damla

Dana
Danae
Danai
Danaya
Daneen
Dani
Dania
Danica
Daniela
Daniele
Daniella
Danielle
Danika
Daniya
Daniyah
Danna
Danni
Danniella
Dannielle
Dannii
Danya
Daphne
Dara
Darasimi
Darby
Darcee
Darcey
Darcey-Leigh
Darcey-Mae
Darcey-Mai
Darcey-May
Darcey-Rae
Darcey-Rose
Darci

Darcia
Darcie
Darcie-Beau
Darcie-Leigh
Darcie-Mae
Darcie-Mai
Darcie-May
Darcie-Rae
Darcie-Rose
Darci-Mai
Darcy
D'arcy
Darcy-Ann
Darcy-Leigh
Darcy-Mae
Darcy-Mai
Darcy-May
Darcy-Rae
Darcy-Rose
Daria
Darija
Darina
Dariya
Darla
Darlene
Darlia
Darshi
Darya
Dasha
Daveena
Davina
Dawn
Daya
Dayana

Dayna
Daytona
Dea
Deanna
Debbie
Debora
Deborah
Deeba
Deedee
Deeksha
Deema
Deena
Deenah
Deeqa
Deetya
Defne
Deimante
Deina
Delaney
Delara
Delcia
Delcie
Delia
Delicia
Delilah
Delilah-Mae
Delilah-May
Delilah-Rose
Delina
Delisha
Della
Delna
Delores
Delphi
Delphie
Delphine
Delta
Delyth
Demelza

Demetra
Demi
Demie
Demi-Lee
Demileigh
Demi-Leigh
Demi-Mae
Demi-Rae
Demi-Rose
Dena
Deni
Denisa
Denise
Denisha
Deniz
Denni
Dennie
Denver
Derin
Desire
Desiree
Despina
Destinee
Destiney
Destiny
Destiny-Rose
Devi
Devina
Devon
Devorah
Devyn
Dexie
Deya
Dhanvi
Dhara
Dhiya
Dhriti
Dhriya
Dhruvi

Dhruvika
Dhwani
Dhyana
Dhyani
Dia
Diala
Diamond
Diana
Diane
Diaz
Dija
Dila
Dilan
Dilara
Dilek
Dileta
Dillon
Dilys
Dima
Dimitra
Dina
Dinah
Dinara
Dini
Dionne
Dior
Diora
Disha
Dishita
Disney
Divina
Divine
Divisha
Divya
Dixie
Diya
Diyana
Diyanah
Djuna

Doaa
Doha
Dolce
Dolcee
Dolci
Dolcie
Dolcie-May
Dollie
Dollie-Mai
Dollie-Rae
Dollie-Rose
Dolly
Dollyanna
Dolly-Anna
Dolly-Mae
Dolly-May
Dolly-Rae
Dolly-Rose
Dominika
Dominique
Donna
Donya
Dora
Dorcas
Dorina
Doris
Dorota
Dorothea
Dorothy
Dottie
Dotty
Dotty-Rose
Dounia
Drew
Drishti
Dua
Duaa
Duha
Dulce
Dulcie
Dulcima
Dunya
Duru
Dusty
Dviti
Dylan
Dzesika

5
NAMES BEGINNING WITH E

Eabha
Eadie
Eady
Ebany
Ebba
Ebonee
Eboni
Ebonie
Ebony
Ebony-Grace
Ebony-Rose
Ebubechukwu
Ebunoluwa
Ecaterina
Ece
Ecem
Echo
Ecrin
Eda
Edee
Eden
Eden-Mae
Eden-Rae
Eden-Rose
Edi
Edie
Edie-Belle
Edie-Mae
Edie-Rose
Edina
Edith
Edith-Rose

Edlyn
Edna
Edyth
Eemaan
Eesha
Eeva
Eevee
Efa
Effie
Effie-Rose
Effy
Efrata
Eibhlin
Eidy
Eila
Eilah
Eileen
Eilidh
Eilish
Eiliyah
Eimaan
Eiman
Eimear
Eira
Eirene
Eirianwen
Eirini
Eirinn
Eirlys
Eirwen
Eirys
Eisha

Eithne
Eiva
Ekam
Ekaterina
Eknoor
Ela
Elaf
Elaha
Elain
Elaina
Elaine
Elan
Elana
Elanna
Elanur
Elara
Elayah
Elayna
Elba
Eldana
Elea
Eleana
Eleanor
Eleanora
Eleanore
Eleanor-Rose
Electra
Eleen
Eleena
Eleeza
Eleina
Eleiyah

Elektra
Elen
Elena
Elena-Mae
Elene
Eleni
Elenora
Elenore
Eleonora
Eleonore
Eleora
Eleri
Elesha
Elexa
Elexis
Eleyana
Eleyna
Elham
Elia
Eliana
Eliane
Elianna
Elianne
Elicia
Elie
Elif
Elifnaz
Elija
Elim
Elin
Elina
Elinor
Eliora
Elis
Elisa
Elisabeta
Elisabeth
Elisabetta

Elise
Elisha
Elisheba
Elisheva
Elisia
Eliska
Elissa
Elissia
Elita
Elitsa
Elivia
Eliya
Eliyah
Eliz
Eliza
Elizabella
Elizabeta
Elizabete
Elizabeth
Elizabeth-May
Elizabeth-Rose
Elizah
Eliza-Louise
Eliza-Mae
Eliza-Mai
Eliza-Rae
Eliza-Rose
Elizaveta
Elize
Elke
Elkie
Ella
Ella-
Ella-Brooke
Ella-Grace
Ellah
Ella-Jade
Ella-Jai
Ella-Jane

Ella-Jayne
Ella-Joy
Ella-Leigh
Ella-Louise
Ellamae
Ella-Mae
Ella-Mai
Ella-Marie
Ellamay
Ella-May
Ellana
Ellara
Ella-Rae
Ella-Rai
Ellaria
Ellarose
Ella-Rose
Elle
Elleanor
Ellee
Ellen
Ellena
Ellenor
Ellen-Rose
Ellese
Elli
Ellia
Elliana
Ellianna
Ellie
Ellie-
Ellie-Ann
Ellie-Anna
Ellie-Grace
Ellie-Jane
Ellie-Jay
Ellie-Jayne
Ellie-Jo
Ellie-Louise

Ellie-Mae
Ellie-Mai
Ellie-Marie
Elliemay
Ellie-May
Ellie-Rae
Ellie-Rose
Elliot
Elliott
Elliotte
Ellis
Ellisa
Ellise
Ellisia
Ellison
Ellissa
Ellissia
Elliw
Ellora
Ellouisa
Ellouise
Ellsie
Elly
Ellyana
Ellys
Ellyse
Ellysia
Elma
Elmas
Elmira
Elna
Elnaz
Eloah
Elodie
Elodie-Mae
Elodie-Rose
Elody
Eloghosa
Eloisa

Eloise
Elona
Elora
Elora-Rose
Elouisa
Elouise
Elowen
Elowyn
Elsa
Elsa-Mae
Elsa-May
Elsa-Rose
Elsbeth
Elsea
Elsey
Elsi
Elsie
Elsie-Ann
Elsie-Anne
Elsie-Grace
Elsie-Jane
Elsie-Jean
Elsie-Leigh
Elsie-Lou
Elsie-Louise
Elsiemae
Elsie-Mae
Elsie-Mai
Elsie-May
Elsie-Rae
Elsie-Rose
Elspeth
Elsy
Eluned
Elva
Elvi
Elvie
Elvin
Elvina

Elvira
Elya
Elyana
Elysa
Elyse
Elysia
Elyssa
Elyssia
Elyza
Elza
Elze
Ema
Emaan
Emalie
Eman
Emanuela
Emanuella
Emaya
Ember
Emeilia
Emel
Emeli
Emelia
Emeliah
Emelia-Mae
Emelia-Rose
Emelie
Emeline
Emely
Emer
Emerald
Emerita
Emerson
Emi
Emie
Emika
Emiko
Emile
Emilee

Emili
Emilia
Emilia-Grace
Emilia-Mae
Emiliana
Emilia-Rose
Emilie
Emilie-Jane
Emilie-Mae
Emilie-Rose
Emilija
Emiliya
Emillia
Emillie
Emilly
Emily
Emilya
Emily-Ann
Emily-Anne
Emily-Grace
Emily-Jane
Emily-Jayne
Emily-Jo
Emily-Mae
Emily-May
Emily-Rae
Emilyrose
Emily-Rose
Emine
Emira
Emma
Emma-Jane
Emma-Leigh
Emmanuela
Emmanuella
Emmanuelle
Emma-Rose
Emme
Emmeline

Emmi
Emmie
Emmie-Leigh
Emmie-Lou
Emmie-Mae
Emmie-Rae
Emmie-Rose
Emmy
Emmylou
Emy
Ena
Enaiya
Enas
Enaya
Eneida
Enfys
Enid
Enija
Eniola
Enisa
Enlli
Enna
Enola
Enrika
Enxi
Enya
Enza
Eowyn
Eponine
Eppie
Era
Erica
Erika
Erin
Erina
Erinn
Erin-Rose
Erioluwa
Eris

Erisa
Erla
Erlisa
Errin
Erum
Erva
Eryka
Eryn
Erynn
Esamae
Esamai
Eseoghene
Eseosa
Esha
Eshaal
Eshal
Eshani
Esher
Esila
Eslem
Esma
Esmae
Esmae-Rose
Esmai
Esmai-Rose
Esmanur
Esmay
Esme
Esmea
Esmee
Esmee-Louise
Esmee-Rose
Esme-Louise
Esme-Rae
Esmeralda
Esmerelda
Esme-Rose
Esmi
Esmia

Esmie
Espen
Esperance
Esra
Essence
Essi
Essia
Essie
Esta
Estee
Estela
Estella
Estelle
Ester
Estera
Estere
Esther
Esti
Estrela
Estrella
Eszter
Etana
Eternity
Ethel
Etienne
Etta
Etta-Mae
Ettie
Ettienne
Etty
Eugenia
Eugenie
Eunice
Euphemia
Eva
Eva-Grace
Evah
Eva-Jean
Eva-Lily

Evalina
Evaline
Eva-Louise
Evalyn
Evalyne
Evalynn
Eva-Mae
Eva-Mai
Eva-Maria
Eva-Marie
Eva-May
Evana
Evangelia
Evangelina
Evangeline
Evanna
Evanthia
Eva-Rose
Eve
Evee
Eveleen
Evelin
Evelina
Eveline
Evelyn
Evelyna
Evelyne
Evelyn-Grace
Evelyn-Mae
Evelyn-May
Evelynn
Evelynne
Evelyn-Rose
Everleigh
Everley
Everlie
Everly
Everlyn
Evi

Evie
Evie-
Evie-Blossom
Eviee
Evie-Grace
Evie-Hope
Evie-Jade
Evie-Jae
Evie-Jai
Evie-Jayne
Evie-Jean
Evie-Lee
Evie-Leigh
Evie-Lou
Evie-Louise
Evie-Lynn
Evie-Mae
Evie-Mai
Evie-Marie
Evie-May
Evie-Rae
Evie-Rose
Evie-Willow
Evin
Evita
Evlyn
Evlynn
Evni
Evony
Evy
Ewa
Ewaoluwa
Ewelina
Exauce
Eydie
Eyla
Eylul
Eysan
Ezgi

Ezinne
Ezmae
Ezmai
Ezmay
Ezme
Ezmee
Ezmie
Ezra
Ezrae
Ezri
Ezzah

6
NAMES BEGINNING WITH F

Faatima
Faatimah
Fabeha
Fabia
Fabiana
Fabiha
Fabiola
Fable
Fadeelah
Fae
Fahima
Fahmida
Faigy
Faiha
Faith
Faiza
Faizah
Fajar
Fajr
Falak
Falaq
Falisha
Fallon
Falon
Fanta
Fara
Farah
Fareedah
Fareeha
Farhana
Farheen
Faria

Fariah
Farida
Faridah
Fariha
Farisha
Farrah
Farryn
Farwa
Farwah
Faryaal
Faryal
Farzana
Fatema
Fathema
Fathima
Fatiha
Fatim
Fatima
Fatimah
Fatimah-Zahra
Fatimah-Zahrah
Fatimatou
Fatima-Zahra
Fatma
Fatou
Fatoumata
Fatoumatta
Fatuma
Fatumata
Fauna
Fausta
Faustina

Faustyna
Favour
Fawn
Fay
Faye
Fayha
Fayrouz
Fayth
Fearn
Fearne
Feigy
Felicia
Felicity
Felicity-Rose
Felicja
Felisha
Fenella
Fern
Fernanda
Ferne
Feyza
Ffion
Fflur
Fia
Fiadh
Fianna
Fifi
Filipa
Filza
Finley
Finn
Finty

Fiona
Fionnuala
Fiorella
Firdaus
Fiyinfoluwa
Fiza
Fizah
Fizza
Fizzah
Flavia
Fleur
Flo
Flora
Floren
Florence
Florence-Rose
Florencia
Florentina
Florentine
Flores
Flori
Floriana
Florie
Florrie
Floryn
Flossie
Flourish
Flynn
Folasade
Fox
Fozia
Fraiya
Frances
Francesca
Francesca-Rose
Francessca
Franchesca
Francheska
Francine

Francisca
Frankee
Franki
Frankie
Frankiee
Frankie-Lee
Frankie-Leigh
Frankie-Mae
Frankie-Mai
Frankie-Marie
Frankie-Rae
Frankie-Rose
Fraya
Frayah
Freda
Frederica
Freida
Freidy
Freja
Freya
Freya-Ann
Freya-Grace
Freyah
Freya-Leigh
Freya-Louise
Freya-Mae
Freya-Mai
Freya-May
Freya-Rose
Freyja
Freyja-Rose
Frida
Frieda
Fruzsina
Fuchsia

7
NAMES BEGINNING WITH G

Gabia
Gabija
Gabriela
Gabriele
Gabriella
Gabrielle
Gaia
Gaja
Gala
Gamze
Gauri
Geet
Gelila
Gemma
Genesis
Genevieve
Georgette
Georgi
Georgia
Georgia-Grace
Georgia-Leigh
Georgia-Louise
Georgia-Mae
Georgia-May
Georgiana
Georgia-Rose
Georgie
Georgie-Mae
Georgie-May
Georgie-Rae
Georgina
Gerda

Gergana
Ghala
Ghina
Gia
Giada
Giana
Gianna
Gigi
Gila
Gillian
Gina
Ginevra
Ginny
Giorgia
Giovanna
Gisele
Giselle
Gittel
Gitty
Giulia
Giuliana
Giulietta
Gizem
Gladys
Gloria
Glorija
Glory
Goda
Goldie
Goldy
Goodness
Grace

Grace-Elizabeth
Grace-Kelly
Gracelyn
Grace-Marie
Gracey
Gracia
Gracie
Gracie-Ann
Gracie-Anne
Gracie-Jane
Gracie-Jo
Gracie-Lee
Gracie-Leigh
Gracie-Lou
Gracie-Louise
Gracie-Mae
Gracie-Mai
Gracie-May
Gracie-Rae
Gracie-Rose
Greta
Gretel
Gretta
Guinevere
Gul
Gulsen
Guneet
Gunes
Gunreet
Gurbani
Gurleen
Gurneet

Gurnoor
Gurpreet
Gurreet
Gurseerat
Gursharan
Gursimran
Gurveen
Guste
Gwen
Gwendoline
Gwendolyn
Gwenllian
Gwenna
Gwennan
Gwenno
Gwyneth
Gypsy
Gypsy-Rose

8
NAMES BEGINNING WITH H

Ha
Haadia
Haadiya
Haadiyah
Haajar
Haajirah
Haajra
Haala
Haania
Haaniya
Haaniyah
Habeeba
Habeebah
Habiba
Habibah
Hadassa
Hadassah
Haddy
Hadeeqa
Hadia
Hadiqa
Hadiya
Hadiyah
Hadley
Hadya
Haf
Hafiza
Hafsa
Hafsah
Haifa
Hailee
Hailey

Hailie
Haiqa
Hajar
Hajara
Hajer
Hajira
Hajirah
Hajra
Hajrah
Hala
Haleema
Haleemah
Hali
Halia
Halima
Halimah
Halina
Halle
Halle-Mae
Halle-Rae
Halli
Hallie
Hallie-Mae
Hallie-May
Hallie-Rae
Hallie-Rose
Hally
Halo
Hamasa
Hamda
Hamna
Hamnah

Han
Hana
Hanaa
Hanah
Hanan
Hanasa
Hanaya
Haneefah
Haneen
Haneet
Hanfa
Hani
Hania
Haniel
Hanifa
Hanifah
Hanife
Haniya
Haniyah
Haniyya
Haniyyah
Hanna
Hannah
Hannah-Mae
Hannah-Marie
Hannah-May
Hannah-Rose
Hannan
Hanni
Hanya
Haram
Harbor

Harbour
Hareem
Hargun
Harini
Harkiran
Harkirat
Harlee
Harleen
Harleigh
Harley
Harley-Mae
Harley-Quinn
Harley-Rose
Harlie
Harlow
Harlowe
Harlow-Rose
Harlyn
Harman
Harmani
Harmanpreet
Harmoni
Harmonie
Harmonie-Rose
Harmony
Harmony-Grace
Harmony-Rose
Harneet
Harnoor
Harper
Harper-Grace
Harper-Jo
Harper-Lee
Harper-Leigh
Harper-Lilly
Harper-Lily
Harper-Louise
Harper-Mae
Harper-Mai

Harper-Rae
Harper-Rose
Harper-Willow
Harpreet
Harri
Harriet
Harriett
Harrietta
Harriette
Harshita
Harsimar
Harsimran
Harveen
Hasanat
Haseena
Hasenat
Hasina
Hasna
Hasti
Hatice
Hatti
Hattie
Hatty
Hava
Havana
Havannah
Haven
Havin
Havva
Hawa
Hawaa
Hawah
Hawwa
Hawwaa
Hawwah
Haya
Hayaa
Hayah
Hayat

Hayden
Hayfa
Haylee
Hayleigh
Hayley
Haylie
Hazal
Hazel
Hazel-Grace
Heather
Heaven
Heavenly
Heba
Hebah
Hebe
Heela
Heer
Heeya
Heidi
Heidi-Leigh
Heidi-Mae
Heidi-Rose
Hela
Helaina
Heleena
Helen
Helena
Helene
Helin
Heloise
Hema
Hena
Henley
Henna
Hennah
Hennessy
Hennie
Henny
Henrietta

Henriette
Hephzibah
Hera
Hermione
Hero
Hessa
Hester
Heti
Hetti
Hettie
Hetty
Hiba
Hibah
Hibba
Hibbah
Hidaya
Hidayah
Hifza
Hijab
Hikmah
Hila
Hilary
Hilda
Hillary
Himani
Hina
Hind
Hinda
Hindy
Hira
Hirah
Hiranur
Hivda
Hiyab
Hiyam
Hoda
Hodan
Holli
Hollie

Hollie-Louise
Hollie-Mae
Hollie-Mai
Hollie-Rose
Holly
Holly-Ann
Holly-Grace
Holly-Mae
Holly-Marie
Holly-May
Holly-Rose
Honey
Honey-Leigh
Honey-Mae
Honey-Rose
Honor
Honour
Hoorain
Hooria
Hooriya
Hooriyah
Hope
Hosana
Hosanna
Houda
Hrisha
Huda
Huma
Humaira
Humairaa
Humairah
Humayra
Humayraa
Humayrah
Humera
Humna
Hunni
Hunnie
Hurain

Husaina
Husna
Husnaa

9

NAMES BEGINNING WITH I

Ianthe	Iliana	Inaara
Iara	Ilinca	Inaaya
Iasmina	Ilithyia	Inaayah
Ibbie	Iliya	Inara
Ibtisam	Iliyana	Inarah
Ibukunoluwa	Iliza	Inas
Ida	Illiana	Inaya
Ida-Rose	Illiyeen	Inayah
Idil	Illyana	Inci
Iesha	Ilma	Indi
Ieva	Ilona	India
Ifeoluwa	Ilsa	Indiah
Ifeoma	Ilwad	Indiana
Ifra	Ilyana	Indianna
Ifrah	Imaan	India-Rose
Ifunanya	Imaani	Indie
Ifza	Iman	Indie-Rae
Iga	Imane	Indie-Rose
Iiyla	Imani	Indigo
Ikhlaas	Imany	Indira
Ikhlas	Imara	Indi-Rae
Ikram	Imarah	Indi-Rose
Ikranur	Imelda	Indiya
Ila	Imelia	Indy
Ilah	Imen	Indya
Ilana	Immy	Ines
Ilaria	Imogen	Inez
Ilayda	Imogen-Hope	Inga
Ileana	Imogen-Louise	Ingrid
Ilhaam	Imogen-Mae	Inika
Ilham	Imogen-Rose	Inioluwa
Ilhan	Ina	Iniya

Inka	Isabella-Grace	Isma
Innaya	Isabella-Mae	Ismah
Innayah	Isabella-Mai	Ismay
Insha	Isabella-May	Isobel
Inshirah	Isabella-Rose	Isobella
Insiya	Isabelle	Isobelle
Intisar	Isabelle-Grace	Isolde
Ioana	Isabelle-Rose	Isra
Ioanna	Isadora	Israa
Iola	Isatou	Israel
Ioli	Isatu	Israh
Iona	Isha	Issabella
Ione	Ishaal	Italia
Ionela	Ishaani	Iudita
Iqra	Ishana	Iulia
Iqrah	Ishani	Iustina
Ira	Ishanvi	Iva
Irah	Ishbel	Ivana
Iraj	Isher	Ivanah
Iram	Ishika	Ivanna
Irem	Ishmeet	Ivayla
Iremide	Ishrat	Iveta
Irene	Isioma	Ivey
Irfa	Isis	Ivie
Irha	Isla	Ivory
Irhaa	Isla-Beau	Ivory-Rose
Irie	Isla-Belle	Ivy
Irina	Isla-Grace	Ivy-Grace
Iris	Islah	Ivy-Leigh
Irisa	Isla-Jane	Ivy-Mae
Iris-Rose	Isla-Lily	Ivy-Marie
Irmak	Isla-Mae	Ivy-May
Irys	Isla-Mai	Ivy-Rae
Isa	Isla-Marie	Ivy-Rose
Isabeau	Isla-May	Iwinosa
Isabel	Isla-Rae	Iyana
Isabela	Isla-Rai	Iyanna
Isabell	Isla-Rose	Iyla
Isabella	Islay	Iylah

Iylah-Mae
Iylah-Rose
Iyla-Mae
Iyla-Rae
Iyla-Rose
Iyobosa
Iyra
Iza
Izabel
Izabela
Izabele
Izabell
Izabella
Izabelle
Izarra
Izel
Izma
Izna
Izobel
Izza
Izzabella
Izzabelle
Izzah
Izzi
Izzie
Izzy

10
NAMES BEGINNING WITH J

Jaanvi
Jacey
Jacinta
Jacqueline
Jada
Jade
Jadzia
Jael
Jagoda
Jahan
Jahnvi
Jahzara
Jaida
Jaime
Jaimee
Jaime-Leigh
Jaimie
Jaina
Jainaba
Jaipreet
Jaiya
Jaiyana
Jaliyah
Jameela
Jameelah
Jamelia
Jamia
Jamie
Jamie-Leigh
Jamila
Jamilah
Jamima

Jana
Janae
Ja'nae
Janan
Janani
Janaya
Jane
Janell
Janelle
Janessa
Janet
Janey
Janiah
Janice
Janina
Janiya
Janiyah
Janna
Jannah
Jannat
Jannath
Jannatul
Jannet
Janvi
Japji
Japneet
Jara
Jasemin
Jasia
Jaskiran
Jaskirat
Jasleen

Jasmeen
Jasmeet
Jasmin
Jasmina
Jasmine
Jasmine-Jade
Jasmine-Rose
Jasminka
Jasmyn
Jasmyne
Jasneet
Jasnoor
Jaspreet
Jasreet
Jasroop
Jasveen
Javeria
Jaweria
Jaya
Jaycee
Jaycee-Leigh
Jaycie
Jayda
Jayde
Jayla
Jaylah
Jaymie
Jaymie-Leigh
Jayna
Jazleen
Jazlyn
Jazmin

Jazmine	Jessica-Louise	Jolanta
Jazmyn	Jessica-Mae	Jolene
Jean	Jessica-Mai	Jolie
Jeanelle	Jessica-May	Jomana
Jeanette	Jessica-Rose	Jona
Jeanie	Jessie	Jonelle
Jeanne	Jessie-Mae	Joni
Jeena	Jessie-May	Jood
Jeevan	Jessika	Jordana
Jeevika	Jessy	Jordanna
Jeeya	Jett	Jordyn
Jemima	Jewel	Jorgi
Jemimah	Jeyda	Jorgia
Jemma	Jhene	Jorgie
Jena	Jia	Jorgie-Mae
Jenessa	Jiana	Jorja
Jenevieve	Jihan	Jorja-Rose
Jenifer	Jimena	Jory
Jenika	Jinan	Joscelyn
Jenisha	Jing	Josefin
Jenna	Jiya	Josefina
Jennah	Jiyana	Joselyn
Jenni	Joan	Josephina
Jennie	Joana	Josephine
Jennifer	Joanie	Josie
Jenny	Joann	Josie-Lea
Jeorgia	Joanna	Josie-Leigh
Jersey	Joanne	Josie-May
Jersie	Jocelyn	Joslyn
Jerusha	Jodi	Joud
Jesica	Jodie	Jouri
Jess	Jody	Joury
Jessa	Joella	Jovie
Jesse	Joelle	Jowita
Jessey	Joely	Joy
Jessi	Joey	Joya
Jessica	Johana	Joyce
Jessica-Jane	Johanna	Juanita
Jessica-Lea	Johannah	Jude

Judi
Judith
Judy
Judyta
Jules
Julia
Juliana
Julianna
Julie
Julienne
Juliet
Julieta
Julietta
Juliette
Julija
Julita
Jumaimah
Juman
Jumana
Jumanah
Jumaymah
Juna
Junaina
Junainah
June
Juniper
Juno
Jupiter
Juri
Justina
Justine
Justyna
Juwairiya
Juwairiyah
Juwariah
Juwariyah
Juwayriah
Juwayriya
Juwayriyah

Juwayriyya
Juweriya
Jwana

11
NAMES BEGINNING WITH K

Kaavya
Kacey
Kacey-Leigh
Kaci
Kacia
Kacie
Kacie-Leigh
Kacie-Mae
Kacie-Rose
Kaci-Leigh
Kaci-Mae
Kaci-Mai
Kacy
Kacy-Leigh
Kaddy
Kadence
Kadey
Kadi
Kadie
Kadie-Mae
Kadija
Kadijah
Kadijatu
Kady
Kaela
Kaelyn
Kaesha
Kahlan
Kaia
Kaida
Kaidence

Kaila
Kaileigh
Kailey
Kailyn
Kainaat
Kainat
Kaira
Kairi
Kaisha
Kaitlin
Kaitlyn
Kaitlynn
Kaitlynne
Kaiya
Kaiyah
Kaja
Kalaya
Kaleesi
Kaley
Kali
Kalila
Kalina
Kalisha
Kaliyah
Kallie
Kalliopi
Kalsoom
Kamara
Kamaya
Kami
Kamiah

Kamila
Kamilah
Kamile
Kamilla
Kamiyah
Kamsiyochukwu
Kana
Kandi
Kaneez
Kani
Kanika
Kanishka
Kanya
Kara
Karah
Kardelen
Kareema
Kareemah
Kareena
Karen
Karenza
Karima
Karin
Karina
Karis
Karisha
Karishma
Karissa
Karla
Karleigh
Karlie

Karma
Karmen
Karolina
Karthika
Karys
Kasandra
Kasey
Kashaf
Kashmala
Kashvi
Kasia
Kasie
Kassandra
Kassidy
Kassie
Katalea
Kataleya
Katalin
Katalina
Katarina
Katarzyna
Kate
Katelin
Katelyn
Katelynn
Katerina
Katey
Katherine
Kathleen
Kathryn
Katia
Katie
Katie-Ann
Katie-Leigh
Katie-Louise
Katie-Mae
Katie-Mai
Katie-May
Katie-Rose

Katja
Katriel
Katrin
Katrina
Katy
Katya
Kausar
Kavleen
Kavya
Kawthar
Kay
Kaya
Kayah
Kayal
Kayan
Kaycee
Kayci
Kaycie
Kaycie-Marie
Kaydee
Kaydi
Kaydie
Kayla
Kaylah
Kayla-Mae
Kayla-May
Kayla-Rose
Kaylee
Kayleigh
Kayley
Kaylie
Kaylin
Kaylla
Kaylyn
Kayna
Kayra
Kaysha
Kaytlin
Kazi

Kazia
Keanna
Keavie
Keavy
Keela
Keeleigh
Keeley
Keely
Keerat
Keeva
Keevah
Kehara
Keiko
Keila
Keira
Keira-Leigh
Keira-Mae
Keira-Rose
Keisha
Keita
Keitija
Kelechi
Kelis
Kellie
Kelly
Kelsea
Kelsey
Kelsey-Mae
Kelsey-Mai
Kelsi
Kelsie
Kelsie-May
Kemi
Kenaya
Kenda
Kendal
Kendall
Kendra
Kenia

Kenna	Khaliyah	Kimberly
Kennedie	Khansa	Kimi
Kennedy	Kharis	Kimia
Kensa	Khatija	Kimmy
Kensi	Khatijah	Kimora
Kenya	Khawla	Kimran
Kenza	Khawlah	Kincso
Kenzi	Khayrah	Kinga
Kenzie	Kheira	Kinjal
Keren	Khiana	Kinsey
Kerensa	Khianna	Kinza
Kerenza	Khirad	Kira
Keris	Khivi	Kirah
Kerry	Khizra	Kiran
Kerry-Ann	Khloe	Kirana
Kerys	Khola	Kirandeep
Kesar	Khrisha	Kirat
Kesha	Khushi	Kirpa
Keshika	Kia	Kirsten
Ketrin	Kiah	Kirstie
Keturah	Kiana	Kirsty
Keya	Kiani	Kiswa
Keyla	Kianna	Kiswah
Keysha	Kiara	Kit
Kezia	Kiarah	Kitana
Keziah	Kiara-Leigh	Kitti
Khadeeja	Kiarna	Kitty
Khadeejah	Kiarra	Kitty-Rose
Khadeja	Kiaya	Kiya
Khadidja	Kiera	Kiyah
Khadija	Kiera-Leigh	Kiyana
Khadijah	Kiera-Rose	Kiyanna
Khadiza	Kierra	Kiyara
Khadra	Kiesha	Kiyla
Khaira	Kiki	Kiyomi
Khaleesi	Kim	Kizzy
Khali	Kimani	Klara
Khalia	Kimaya	Klaudia
Khalisa	Kimberley	Klaudija

Klea
Kleo
Kloe
Kodi
Kodie
Komal
Konnie
Kora
Kori
Kornelia
Korra
Kosisochukwu
Kotryna
Kourtney
Krina
Krisha
Krishna
Krishti
Krisia
Krisiya
Krista
Kristal
Kristen
Kristin
Kristina
Kristine
Kriti
Krystal
Krystal-Rose
Ksenia
Ksenija
Kseniya
Kubra
Kulsoom
Kulsum
Kumba
Kushi
Kya
Kyah

Kyara
Kyla
Kylah
Kyla-Mae
Kyla-Rose
Kylie
Kymora
Kyna
Kyomi
Kyra
Kyrah
Kyra-Leigh
Kyra-May
Kyra-Rose

12
NAMES BEGINNING WITH L

Laaibah
Labeebah
Labiba
Lacee
Lacey
Lacey-Grace
Lacey-Jane
Lacey-Jay
Lacey-Jayne
Lacey-Jo
Lacey-Lee
Lacey-Leigh
Lacey-Lou
Lacey-Louise
Lacey-Mae
Lacey-Mai
Lacey-Marie
Lacey-May
Lacey-Rae
Lacey-Rose
Laci
Lacie
Lacie-Leigh
Lacie-Mae
Lacie-Mai
Lacie-Marie
Lacie-May
Lacie-Rose
Lacy
Lady
Lael
Laela

Laelia
Laetitia
Lahna
Laia
Laiba
Laibah
Laicee
Laiha
Laiken
Laila
Laila-Grace
Lailah
Laila-Mae
Laila-Mai
Laila-May
Laila-Rae
Laila-Rose
Laina
Laine
Lainee
Lainey
Lainey-Rae
Lainie
Laiya
Lake
Lakshana
Lakshmi
Lalita
Lama
Lamaisah
Lamar
Lamees

Lamia
Lamis
Lamisa
Lamisah
Lamiya
Lamorna
Lamya
Lana
Lanah
Lana-Rose
Laney
Lani
Lania
Lanie
Lano
Lany
Lanya
Lara
La'rae
Laraib
Lara-Jade
Lara-Mae
Laranya
Lara-Rose
Lareen
Larin
Larisa
Larissa
Larna
Larnie
Larosa
Lataya

Latifa
Latifah
Latin
Latisha
Latoya
Laura
Laurel
Laurelle
Lauren
Laurie
Lavanya
Laveah
Lavender
Lavin
Lavinia
Laya
Layaan
Layah
Layal
Layan
Layanah
Laycee
Laycie
Layla
Layla-Ann
Layla-Belle
Layla-Grace
Laylah
Layla-Jai
Layla-Jane
Layla-Jay
Layla-Jayne
Layla-Jean
Layla-Leigh
Layla-Louise
Layla-Mae
Layla-Mai
Layla-Marie
Layla-May

Layla-Rae
Layla-Rose
Layna
Laynie
Layyanah
Lea
Leah
Leah-Marie
Leah-May
Leah-Rose
Leala
Leana
Leandra
Leanna
Leanne
Leea
Leela
Leelah
Leela-Rose
Leen
Leena
Leenah
Leeya
Leia
Leigh
Leigha
Leighanna
Leighla
Leila
Leila-Grace
Leilah
Leila-Mae
Leila-Mai
Leila-Marie
Leila-May
Leilani
Leila-Rose
Leilia
Leire

Leisha
Leja
Lejla
Lela
Lelia
Leliana
Lema
Lemar
Lena
Leni
Lenia
Lenka
Lenna
Lenni
Lennie
Lennon
Lennox
Lenny
Lenox
Leola
Leona
Leoni
Leonie
Leonor
Leonora
Leonore
Leora
Lerryn
Lesley
Leticia
Letisha
Letisia
Letitia
Letti
Lettie
Letty
Levana
Levi
Lewa

Lewan	Lianna	Lilija
Lexa	Lianne	Lili-Mae
Lexi	Liara	Lili-Mai
Lexi-Ann	Liarna	Lilith
Lexi-Anne	Liba	Liliya
Lexie	Libbi	Lilja
Lexie-Grace	Libbie	Lilla
Lexie-Leigh	Libby	Lillee
Lexie-Louise	Libby-Mae	Lilley
Lexie-Mae	Libby-Rose	Lilley-Mae
Lexie-Mai	Liberty	Lilli
Lexie-Rae	Liberty-Rose	Lillia
Lexie-Rose	Lidia	Lilliah
Lexi-Grace	Lidya	Lillian
Lexii	Lielle	Lilliana
Lexi-Jayne	Liepa	Lilli-Ann
Lexi-Lee	Ligia	Lillianna
Lexi-Leigh	Lila	Lilli-Anne
Lexi-Lou	Lilac	Lilliarna
Lexi-Louise	Lila-Grace	Lillia-Rose
Lexi-Mae	Lilah	Lillibeth
Lexi-Mai	Lilah-Mae	Lillie
Lexi-Marie	Lilah-Mai	Lillie-Ann
Lexi-May	Lilah-Rose	Lillie-Anna
Lexi-Rae	Lila-Mae	Lillie-Anne
Lexi-Rose	Lila-Rose	Lillie-Ella
Lexis	Lilee	Lillie-Grace
Lexus	Lili	Lillie-Mae
Lexy	Lilia	Lillie-Mai
Leya	Liliah	Lillie-Marie
Leyah	Lilian	Lillie-May
Leyan	Liliana	Lillie-Rae
Leyana	Liliane	Lillierose
Leyla	Lilianna	Lillie-Rose
Leylah	Lilianne	Lillith
Leyna	Lilian-Rose	Lilly
Lia	Lilia-Rose	Lillyana
Lian	Lilibeth	Lillyann
Liana	Lilien	Lilly-Ann

Lillyanna
Lilly-Anna
Lillyanne
Lilly-Anne
Lilly-Ella
Lilly-Grace
Lilly-Jane
Lilly-Jayne
Lilly-Jo
Lillymae
Lilly-Mae
Lilly-Mai
Lilly-Marie
Lillymay
Lilly-May
Lilly-Rae
Lillyrose
Lilly-Rose
Lilou
Lily
Lily-
Lilya
Lilyana
Lily-Ann
Lilyanna
Lily-Anna
Lilyanne
Lily-Anne
Lilybelle
Lily-Belle
Lilybeth
Lily-Ella
Lily-Eve
Lily-Faith
Lily-Grace
Lily-Hope
Lily-Jane
Lily-Jayne
Lily-Jean

Lily-Jo
Lily-Louise
Lilymae
Lily-Mae
Lily-Mai
Lily-Marie
Lily-May
Lily-Rae
Lily-Rose
Lily-Sue
Lina
Linda
Lindsay
Lindsey
Ling
Linh
Linnea
Liora
Lisa
Lisa-Marie
Lisbeth
Lisha
Lissi
Lissie
Lissy
Liv
Livi
Livia
Liviah
Livie
Livinia
Livvi
Livvie
Livvy
Livy
Liwia
Liwsi
Liya
Liyaa

Liyaana
Liyaanah
Liyah
Liyan
Liyana
Liyanah
Liylah
Liz
Liza
Lizzie
Lizzy
Llana
Lleucu
Llinos
Llio
Logan
Lois
Lojain
Lola
Lola-Belle
Lola-Grace
Lolah
Lola-Jade
Lola-Jane
Lola-Louise
Lola-Mae
Lola-Mai
Lola-Marie
Lola-May
Lola-Rae
Lola-Rose
Lolita
Lolly
Lona
London
Lora
Lordina
Loredana
Lorelai

Lorelei
Lorella
Loren
Lorena
Lorenna
Loresa
Loreta
Loretta
Lori
Lorien
Lorin
Lorna
Lorraine
Loti
Lotta
Lotte
Lotti
Lottie
Lottie-Leigh
Lottie-Lou
Lottie-Louise
Lottie-Mae
Lottie-May
Lottie-Rae
Lottie-Rose
Lotty
Lotus
Lou
Louanne
Louella
Louisa
Louise
Louisiana
Loula
Lourdes
Love
Lovelle
Lowen
Lowena

Lowenna
Lowri
Lua
Luana
Luanna
Lubabah
Lubna
Luca
Lucca
Lucea
Luchia
Luci
Lucia
Luciana
Lucianna
Lucie
Lucie-Mae
Lucie-Mai
Lucienne
Lucille
Lucinda
Lucja
Lucy
Lucy-Ann
Lucy-Anne
Lucy-Jo
Lucy-Lou
Lucy-Mae
Lucy-May
Lucy-Rae
Lucy-Rose
Luella
Luena
Luisa
Luiza
Luize
Lujain
Lujane
Luka

Lukrecja
Lula
Lulabelle
Lulah
Lullah
Lulu
Lulua
Lumen
Lumi
Luna
Luna-Belle
Luna-Mae
Luna-May
Lunar
Luna-Rae
Luna-Rose
Lura
Lusia
Luul
Lux
L'wren
Lya
Lyana
Lyanna
Lyara
Lycia
Lydia
Lydia-Mae
Lydia-May
Lydia-Rose
Lyla
Lyla-Belle
Lyla-Grace
Lylah
Lylah-Rose
Lyla-Mae
Lyla-Rae
Lyla-Rose
Lylia

BABY GIRL NAMES

Lynn
Lyra
Lyrah
Lyra-May
Lyra-Rose
Lyric
Lyza

13
NAMES BEGINNING WITH M

Maahi
Maahnoor
Maame
Maanvi
Maanya
Maaria
Maariya
Maariyah
Maarya
Maayan
Mabel
Mabelle
Mable
Mabli
Macey
Macey-Leigh
Macey-May
Maci
Macie
Macie-Lea
Macie-Leigh
Macie-Lou
Macie-Mae
Macie-Rae
Maci-Lea
Maci-Rae
Mackenzie
Macy
Macy-Rae
Macy-Rose
Madalena
Madalina

Madaline
Madalyn
Maddi
Maddie
Maddie-Leigh
Maddison
Maddison-Grace
Maddison-Leigh
Maddison-Mae
Maddison-May
Maddison-Rae
Maddison-Rose
Maddy
Madeeha
Madelaine
Madeleine
Madeline
Madelyn
Madelyne
Madi
Madiha
Madihah
Madilyn
Madina
Madinah
Madison
Madison-Mae
Madisson
Madisyn
Madyson
Mae
Maebh

Maeby
Maeesha
Maelys
Maeva
Maeve
Maeya
Mafalda
Magda
Magdalena
Magdalene
Maggi
Maggie
Maggie-Ann
Maggie-Mae
Maggie-May
Maggie-Rose
Magi
Magnolia
Maha
Mahalia
Maham
Mahathi
Mahdia
Mahdiya
Mahdiyah
Mahee
Maheen
Maheera
Mahek
Mahi
Mahia
Mahibah

Mahika
Mahima
Mahira
Mahisha
Mahiya
Mahjabin
Mahla
Mahlia
Mahnaz
Mahnoor
Mahnur
Mahreen
Mahrosh
Mahrukh
Mahsa
Mahum
Mai
Maia
Maiah
Maia-Rose
Maicee
Maicey
Maicie
Maida
Maidah
Maija
Maila
Maily
Maimuna
Mair
Maira
Mairah
Mairead
Mairi
Maisey
Maisha
Maisie
Maisie-
Maisie-Anne

Maisie-Grace
Maisie-Jane
Maisie-Jayne
Maisie-Jean
Maisie-Lea
Maisie-Lee
Maisie-Leigh
Maisie-Lou
Maisie-Mai
Maisie-May
Maisie-Rae
Maisie-Rose
Maisy
Maisy-Leigh
Maitri
Maiya
Maiyah
Maiza
Maizee
Maizey
Maizie
Maizy
Maja
Majida
Majka
Makanaka
Makayla
Makeda
Makenna
Mala
Malaak
Malaika
Malaikah
Malak
Malala
Malaya
Malayah
Malaysia
Maleah

Maleeha
Maleeka
Maleka
Malena
Malgorzata
Mali
Malia
Maliah
Maliha
Malika
Malikah
Malina
Maliya
Maliyah
Malka
Malky
Mallory
Mally
Malvika
Malwina
Mamie
Manaal
Manahal
Manahel
Manahil
Manal
Manar
Manasa
Manasvi
Manat
Mandy
Manel
Manha
Manisha
Mankirat
Manmeet
Mannat
Manon
Manreet

Manroop	Mariam	Marlie
Mansirat	Mariama	Marlie-Mae
Mantasha	Marian	Marlow
Manuela	Mariana	Marlowe
Manuella	Marianna	Marly
Manvi	Marianne	Marney
Manya	Marie	Marni
Maple	Mariel	Marnie
Mara	Mariella	Marnie-Mai
Maram	Marielle	Marnie-Rae
Maranatha	Mariem	Marnie-Rose
Maraya	Marigold	Marta
Marcelina	Marija	Martha
Marceline	Marika	Martha-Rose
Marcella	Marilena	Martina
Marcey	Marilyn	Martyna
Marci	Marin	Marvellous
Marcia	Marina	Marvelous
Marcie	Marion	Marwa
Marcie-Mae	Marisa	Marwah
Marcy	Marissa	Marwo
Mardiya	Marita	Mary
Mared	Marium	Marya
Mareen	Mariya	Maryam
Marella	Mariyah	Maryama
Maren	Mariyam	Maryan
Margaret	Mariyyah	Maryann
Margarida	Marketa	Mary-Ann
Margarita	Marla	Maryanne
Margaux	Marlea	Mary-Anne
Marged	Marlee	Maryjane
Margherita	Marlee-Mae	Mary-Jane
Margo	Marleigh	Mary-Jayne
Margot	Marlena	Mary-Kate
Marguerite	Marlene	Marylou
Mari	Marley	Maryrose
Maria	Marley-Mae	Mary-Rose
Mariah	Marley-Rae	Marysia
Maria-Lily	Marli	Maryum

Masa	Maysa	Mehnoor
Masal	Maysam	Mehr
Mashal	Maysarah	Mehrab
Masie	Maysie	Mehreen
Masooma	Maysoon	Mehrish
Massa	Mayssa	Mehvish
Masuma	Mayzee	Mehwish
Mathilda	Mayzie	Mei
Mathilde	Mazie	Meida
Matilda	Mckayla	Meila
Matilda-Rose	Mckenna	Meira
Matilde	Mckenzie	Meisha
Matty	Mea	Meklit
Matylda	Meabh	Mela
Maud	Meadow	Melani
Maude	Meagan	Melania
Maureen	Meah	Melanie
Mavis	Meda	Melanija
Mawa	Medi	Melany
Mawadda	Medina	Melek
Maxie	Medine	Melia
Maxine	Meela	Melika
May	Meena	Melike
Maya	Meenakshi	Melina
Mayah	Meera	Melinda
Mayar	Meerab	Melis
Mayara	Meesha	Melisa
Maya-Rose	Meeya	Melissa
Maybelle	Meg	Melita
Mayci	Megan	Mellissa
Maycie	Megan-Rose	Melodie
Mayeda	Megha	Melody
Mayla	Meghan	Melody-May
Mayle	Megija	Melody-Rose
Maylee	Mehak	Memphis
Maylie	Mehar	Mena
Maymuna	Mehek	Menaal
Maymunah	Meher	Menna
Mayra	Mehjabeen	Mercedes

Mercy	Micaela	Milla
Meredith	Micah	Millee
Meriam	Micayla	Miller
Merida	Michaela	Milli
Meriem	Michaella	Millicent
Merilin	Michal	Millie
Merilyn	Michalina	Millie-Ann
Merle	Michela	Millie-Anne
Merrin	Michella	Millie-Grace
Merry	Michelle	Millie-Jo
Merryn	Michle	Millie-Leigh
Merve	Midori	Millie-Louise
Merveille	Mieke	Millie-Mae
Meryem	Miesha	Millie-Mai
Meryl	Migle	Millie-Marie
Meryn	Mihaela	Millie-May
Meta	Mihika	Millie-Rae
Meya	Mija	Millie-Rose
Mhairi	Mika	Milly
Mia	Mikaela	Milly-Mae
Mia-Anne	Mikayla	Milly-May
Miabella	Mila	Milly-Rose
Mia-Bella	Mila-Grace	Mimi
Mia-Grace	Milagros	Mina
Miah	Milah	Minaal
Mia-Jade	Milan	Minahil
Mia-Jane	Milana	Minal
Mia-Jayne	Milani	Mindy
Mia-Leigh	Milania	Minerva
Mia-Lilly	Milanna	Minha
Mia-Lily	Mila-Rae	Minka
Mia-Louise	Mila-Rose	Minna
Mia-Mae	Milda	Minnah
Mia-May	Milena	Minnie
Miami	Miley	Minnie-Mae
Mia-Rae	Miley-Rose	Minnie-Rae
Miarose	Mili	Minnie-Rose
Mia-Rose	Miliana	Minny
Mica	Milita	Minsa

Mio
Mira
Mirab
Mirabel
Mirabelle
Miracle
Miral
Miranda
Miray
Miraya
Mirel
Mirella
Mireya
Mirha
Miri
Miriam
Miroslava
Mirren
Miruna
Misa
Misaki
Misbah
Mischa
Misha
Mishaal
Mishal
Mishika
Mishka
Missie
Missy
Misty
Mitzi
Mitzie
Miya
Miyah
Miyah-Rose
Miyla
Mmesomachukwu
Modesire

Modesireoluwa
Mofiyinfoluwa
Mojolaoluwa
Moksha
Moli
Mollie
Mollie-Anne
Mollie-Mae
Mollie-Mai
Mollie-Rae
Mollie-Rose
Molly
Molly-Jane
Molly-Mae
Molly-Mai
Molly-May
Molly-Rose
Momina
Mominah
Momoko
Mona
Monae
Monalisa
Monet
Monica
Monika
Monique
Monira
Monroe
Montana
Morayo
Morena
Morgan
Morgana
Moriah
Morrigan
Morwenna
Moya
Moyinoluwa

Mozan
Muireann
Mumina
Muminah
Mumtaz
Muna
Munachimso
Muneefa
Muneerah
Muniba
Munira
Munirat
Muntaha
Muntaz
Muqadas
Muqaddas
Murphy
Muska
Muskaan
Muskan
Mutsa
Mya
Mya-Grace
Myah
Myah-Rose
Mya-Louise
Myanna
Mya-Rae
Mya-Rose
Myer
Myfi
Myia
Myiah
Myiesha
Myka
Myla
Mylah
Mylah-Rose
Myla-Mae

Myla-May
Myla-Rae
Myla-Rose
Mylee
Myleene
Myleigh
Mylie
Myra
Myrah
Myriam
Myrtle
Mysha

14
NAMES BEGINNING WITH N

Naa
Naairah
Naavya
Naba
Nabeeha
Nabeela
Nabeelah
Nabia
Nabiha
Nabihah
Nabila
Nacera
Nada
Nadejda
Nadezhda
Nadia
Nadine
Nadira
Nadiya
Nadya
Naeema
Naeemah
Naevia
Nafeesa
Nafeesah
Nafisa
Nafisah
Nahia
Nahla
Naia
Naiara
Naida

Naila
Nailah
Naima
Naimah
Naina
Nainika
Naira
Nairah
Naisha
Naiya
Naiyah
Najia
Najma
Najwa
Nakshatra
Nala
Nalah
Nalani
Naledi
Nameera
Namirah
Nana
Nanci
Nancie
Nancy
Nancy-Jane
Nancy-Leigh
Nancy-Mae
Nancy-May
Nancy-Rose
Nandin
Nandini

Nanki
Nansi
Naoise
Naomi
Naomi-Rose
Nara
Narcisa
Nardos
Nariah
Narin
Nariyah
Narjis
Narla
Narmin
Naseeha
Nasma
Nasra
Nasreen
Nasteha
Natalia
Natalie
Natalija
Natalina
Nataliya
Nataly
Natalya
Natania
Natasa
Natasha
Natasza
Nathalia
Nathalie

Nathania	Nefeli	Nevaeh-Rose
Naureen	Nefertari	Nevaya
Navayah	Neha	Nevayah
Naveah	Nehal	Neve
Naveena	Nehir	Neveah
Navkirat	Neive	Neya
Navleen	Nel	Nia
Navneet	Nela	Niah
Navpreet	Neli	Nialah
Navreet	Nelia	Niamh
Navya	Nell	Niara
Nawaal	Nella	Nicki
Nawal	Nelle	Nico
Naya	Nelli	Nicol
Nayab	Nellie	Nicola
Nayah	Nellie-Mae	Nicole
Nayara	Nellie-Rae	Nicoleta
Nayla	Nellie-Rose	Nicoll
Naylaa	Nelly	Nicolle
Naylah	Nelly-Rae	Nida
Nayra	Nelly-Rose	Nidhi
Naysa	Nena	Nieve
Naysha	Nene	Nigella
Naz	Neraya	Nihal
Nazia	Nerea	Niharika
Nazifa	Neriah	Nika
Naziha	Neriyah	Niki
Nazira	Nerys	Nikita
Nazli	Nese	Nikki
Nazmin	Nessa	Nikkita
Nea	Nesta	Niko
Neave	Nethra	Nikol
Nechama	Nettie	Nikola
Nectaria	Neva	Nikole
Neda	Nevaeh	Nikolett
Neela	Nevaeh-Grace	Nila
Neeva	Nevaeh-Mai	Nilah
Neevah	Nevaeh-Marie	Nimco
Neeve	Nevaeh-Rae	Nimra

Nimrah
Nimrat
Nimrit
Nimrita
Nina
Niniola
Niomi
Nirvair
Nirvana
Nirvi
Nisa
Nisha
Nishika
Nishka
Nisreen
Nissi
Nitasha
Nitya
Niva
Nixie
Niya
Niyah
Niyat
Niyati
Niyla
Niylah
Nkechi
Nma
Nneka
Nnenna
Noa
Noah
Noami
Noelia
Noella
Noelle
Noemi
Noemie
Noha

Nola
Nolah
Non
Noomi
Noor
Noora
Noor-Fatima
Nooriya
Noorjahan
Noorulain
Noor-Ul-Ain
Nora
Norah
Noreen
Nori
Norina
Nouf
Nour
Noura
Nourah
Noureen
Nova
Novah
Novalee
Novella
Nuala
Nuha
Nuhaa
Nula
Nuo
Nur
Nura
Nurah
Nuran
Nuray
Nuria
Nuriyah
Nusaiba
Nusaibah

Nusayba
Nusaybah
Nusrat
Nuwaira
Nya
Nyah
Nyasha
Nyasia
Nyla
Nylah
Nylah-Rose
Nyla-Rae
Nyla-Rose
Nyra
Nyree
Nysa
Nysha
Nyx

15
NAMES BEGINNING WITH O

Oaklea
Oakleigh
Oakley
Ocean
Oceana
Oceane
Oceania
Oceanna
Ocean-Rose
Octavia
Odelia
Odette
Odrija
Ofelia
Ogechukwu
Oghenetega
Ohana
Ola
Olachi
Olamide
Olanna
Olayemi
Olenka
Olga
Olimpia
Olive
Olive-Rose
Olivia
Olivia-Faith
Olivia-Grace
Olivia-Jade
Olivia-Jane

Olivia-Jean
Olivia-Leigh
Olivia-Louise
Olivia-Mae
Olivia-Mai
Olivia-Marie
Olivia-May
Olivia-Rae
Olivia-Rose
Olivija
Oliwia
Oluchi
Oluwabukola
Oluwadamilola
Oluwadarasimi
Oluwajomiloju
Oluwakemi
Oluwanifemi
Oluwasemilore
Oluwatamilore
Oluwatimileyin
Oluwatobiloba
Oluwatomi
Oluwatomiwa
Oluwatoni
Olwen
Olympia
Omaima
Omera
Omisha
Omnia
Omolola

Omotara
Omotola
Ona
Onora
Onyinyechi
Onyinyechukwu
Oona
Oonagh
Opal
Ophelia
Ora
Oreofeoluwa
Oreoluwa
Oriana
Oriane
Orianna
Oriella
Orissa
Orla
Orlagh
Orlah
Orlaith
Orla-Mae
Orla-Rose
Orli
Orly
Ornela
Ornella
Osarugue
Oshun
Otilia
Ottilia

Ottilie
Ottoline
Otylia
Oumou
Oviya
Oyindamola
Oyinkansola
Oyku

16
NAMES BEGINNING WITH P

Paige
Paighton
Paignton
Paislee
Paisleigh
Paisley
Paisley-Grace
Paisley-Mai
Paisley-Rae
Paloma
Pamela
Pandora
Panna
Paola
Pareesa
Pari
Paridhi
Paris
Parisa
Parisha
Parishay
Parishi
Parker
Parker-Rose
Parneet
Parnika
Parveen
Parya
Pascale
Patience
Patricia
Patricija

Patrisia
Patrycja
Patsy
Patti
Paula
Paulina
Pauline
Pavan
Pavithra
Pavneet
Payton
Payton-Grace
Paz
Peace
Peaches
Pearl
Pebbles
Peggie
Peggy
Peggy-Mae
Peighton
Penda
Penelope
Penelope-Rose
Pennie
Penny
Penny-Rose
Peony
Pepper
Perdita
Perez
Peri

Perla
Perri
Perrie
Perrie-Rose
Perry
Persephone
Persia
Pessy
Peta
Petal
Petra
Peyton
Peyton-Leigh
Peyton-Rose
Phaedra
Phebe
Pheobe
Pheobie
Phia
Philippa
Phillipa
Phillippa
Philomena
Phoebe
Phoebe-Grace
Phoebe-Jo
Phoebe-Leigh
Phoebe-Mae
Phoebe-Mai
Phoebe-Rae
Phoebe-Rose
Phoebie

Phoenix
Phoenix-Rose
Phoenyx
Pia
Pihu
Pip
Piper
Piper-Rose
Pippa
Pippa-Rose
Pippi
Pixie
Pixie-Lou
Pixie-Mae
Pixie-Rae
Piya
Pola
Polina
Pollie
Polly
Pollyanna
Polly-Anna
Poppi
Poppie
Poppie-Mae
Poppy
Poppy-Ann
Poppy-Belle
Poppy-Grace
Poppy-Jo
Poppy-Leigh
Poppy-Louise
Poppy-Mae
Poppy-Mai
Poppy-Marie
Poppy-May
Poppy-Rae
Poppy-Rose
Porscha

Porsche
Porsche-Leigh
Porsha
Porsha-Leigh
Portia
Posey
Posy
Prabh
Prabhgun
Prabhjot
Prabhkirat
Prabhleen
Prabhnoor
Praise
Pranati
Pranavi
Pranaya
Precious
Preesha
Preet
Preeya
Presha
Presley
Pria
Primrose
Princess
Princy
Prisca
Priscilla
Prisha
Pritika
Priya
Priyana
Priyanka
Priyanshi
Promise
Prudence
Prue
Pudding

Purdy
Purity
Purvi
Pyper

17
NAMES BEGINNING WITH Q

Qirat
Qudsia
Queenie
Quincy
Quinn
Quorra

18
NAMES BEGINNING WITH R

Raahima
Raaina
Raameen
Raaya
Rabia
Rabiah
Rabiya
Rachael
Racheal
Rachel
Radeyah
Radha
Radhika
Radiya
Radiyah
Radoslava
Rae
Raeesa
Raegan
Raelle
Raena
Raeven
Raeya
Rafaela
Rafaella
Rafeef
Raffaella
Raghad
Raha
Rahaf
Raheema
Rahel

Rahela
Rahil
Rahima
Rahma
Rahmah
Rahmeen
Raia
Raiah
Raihana
Raima
Rain
Raina
Raine
Raisa
Raissa
Raiya
Raiyah
Rajvi
Rakeb
Raluca
Rameen
Ramisa
Ramla
Ramlah
Ramneek
Ramona
Rana
Randa
Raneem
Rani
Rania
Raniya

Ranya
Raphaela
Raphaella
Raphaelle
Raquel
Raseel
Rateel
Raven
Ravenna
Ravleen
Ravneet
Rawan
Rawdah
Raya
Rayaan
Rayah
Rayan
Rayana
Rayann
Rayanna
Rayhana
Rayna
Rayne
Raysa
Rayssa
Rayya
Rayyan
Raz
Razaan
Razan
Rea
Reagan

Reanna	Remiah	Rhiannon
Reba	Remie	Rhoda
Rebeca	Remington	Rhona
Rebecca	Remy	Rhoswen
Rebeka	Ren	Ria
Rebekah	Rena	Riah
Rebekkah	Renad	Rian
Red	Renae	Riana
Ree	Renai	Rianna
Reegan	Renata	Rianne
Reeha	Renay	Richelle
Reem	Renaya	Rida
Reema	Renayah	Riddhi
Reena	Renaye	Ridha
Reenie	Rene	Ridhi
Reese	Renea	Ridhima
Reet	Renee	Rifky
Reetal	Renesmae	Riham
Reeva	Renesmai	Rihan
Reeya	Renesmay	Rihana
Regan	Renesme	Rihanah
Regina	Renesmee	Rihanna
Reha	Renezmae	Rijja
Reham	Renna	Rikki
Rehana	Retaj	Riley
Rehmat	Retal	Riley-Mae
Rei	Reva	Rim
Reign	Revah	Rima
Reilly	Reya	Rimas
Reina	Reyah	Rimsha
Reisel	Reyhana	Rina
Reisy	Reyna	Rinad
Reizel	Rhea	Rini
Reka	Rhema	Rinnah
Rema	Rheya	Rio
Remae	Rhia	Riona
Remas	Rhian	Ripley
Remaya	Rhianna	Risha
Remi	Rhianne	Rishika

Rishita
Rita
Ritaj
Rithika
Ritika
Ritisha
Ritvi
Riva
River
River-Leigh
River-Mae
River-Rose
Rivka
Rivkah
Rivky
Riya
Riyaan
Riyah
Riyan
Riyana
Rizwana
Roaa
Roberta
Robin
Robyn
Robyn-Rae
Rochel
Rochelle
Rodina
Rogue
Rohey
Roisin
Roja
Rojin
Roksana
Roma
Romaisa
Romana
Romany

Romaya
Romeesa
Romessa
Romey
Romi
Romilly
Romily
Romina
Romy
Rona
Roni
Ronia
Ronika
Ronja
Ronni
Ronnie
Ronnie-Leigh
Ronnie-Mae
Ronnie-May
Roohi
Roop
Rory
Rosa
Rosabella
Rosa-Bella
Rosabelle
Rosalea
Rosa-Lea
Rosalee
Rosaleigh
Rosa-Leigh
Rosalia
Rosalie
Rosalina
Rosalind
Rosalyn
Rosamund
Rosanna
Rose

Roseann
Roseanna
Roseanne
Roseleen
Rosella
Roselyn
Rosemarie
Rose-Marie
Rosemary
Rosetta
Rosey
Rosha
Roshni
Rosie
Rosie-Ann
Rosie-Anne
Rosie-Grace
Rosie-Jane
Rosie-Lee
Rosie-Leigh
Rosie-Lou
Rosie-Louise
Rosie-Mae
Rosie-Mai
Rosie-Marie
Rosie-May
Rosina
Rosy
Roux
Rowan
Rowanne
Rowen
Rowena
Rowenna
Roxana
Roxanna
Roxanne
Roxie
Roxy

Roxy-Leigh
Roya
Roza
Rozalia
Rua
Ruba
Rubab
Rubani
Rubi
Rubie
Rubie-Leigh
Rubie-Louise
Rubie-Mae
Rubi-Mae
Rubina
Ruby
Ruby-Ann
Ruby-Anne
Ruby-Grace
Ruby-Jane
Ruby-Jayne
Ruby-Jean
Ruby-Jo
Ruby-Lea
Ruby-Lee
Ruby-Leigh
Ruby-Lou
Ruby-Louise
Ruby-Mae
Ruby-Mai
Ruby-Marie
Ruby-May
Ruby-Rae
Ruby-Rose
Ruchi
Rudi
Rudie
Rudo
Rue

Rufaida
Rugile
Ruhama
Ruhani
Ruhi
Ruhina
Rukaiya
Rukaya
Rukayah
Rukia
Rukiya
Rumaisa
Rumaisah
Rumaysa
Rumaysaa
Rumaysah
Rumer
Rumeysa
Rumi
Runa
Ruo
Ruqaiya
Ruqaiyah
Ruqaiyya
Ruqaiyyah
Ruqaya
Ruqayah
Ruqayya
Ruqayyah
Ruqqayah
Rushda
Rushika
Rusne
Rut
Ruta
Ruth
Ruvarashe
Ruwaida
Ruwayda

Ruweyda
Ruya
Rya
Ryah
Ryan
Ryla
Rylea
Rylee
Ryleigh
Rylie
Rym

19
NAMES BEGINNING WITH S

Saachi
Saadia
Saadiya
Saairah
Saaliha
Saalihah
Saanvi
Saara
Saarah
Saavi
Saba
Sabaa
Sabah
Sabeeha
Sabeeka
Sabeen
Sabella
Sabiha
Sabina
Sabine
Sabirin
Sabreen
Sabrin
Sabrina
Sabriyah
Sacha
Sadaf
Sadan
Sade
Sadia
Sadie
Sadie-Mae

Sadie-Rae
Sadiya
Sadiyah
Saeeda
Safa
Safaa
Safah
Safeerah
Safeeya
Saffa
Saffah
Saffi
Saffia
Saffie
Saffire
Saffiya
Saffiyah
Saffron
Safia
Safina
Safira
Safire
Safiya
Safiyah
Safiye
Safiyya
Safiyyah
Safoora
Safoorah
Saga
Sagal
Sage

Sahana
Sahar
Sahara
Saharah
Sahasra
Sahej
Sahib
Sahiba
Sahira
Sahra
Sai
Saiba
Saida
Saifa
Saige
Saima
Saina
Sainabou
Saira
Sairah
Saisha
Saja
Sajida
Sakeena
Sakeenah
Sakina
Sakinah
Sakura
Saleena
Saleha
Saliha
Salihah

Salima
Salina
Sally
Salma
Salmah
Salome
Salsabeel
Salwa
Sama
Samaa
Samah
Samaira
Samaiya
Saman
Samanta
Samantha
Samanvi
Samar
Samara
Samarah
Samaya
Sameeha
Sameera
Sameerah
Samia
Samiah
Samiha
Samina
Samira
Samirah
Samiya
Samiyah
Sammie
Samra
Samrah
Samrawit
Samreen
Samreet
Samuela

Sana
Sanaa
Sanah
Sanam
Sanaya
Sanayah
Sanchia
Sancia
Sandra
Sandy
Sania
Saniya
Saniyah
Saniyya
Sanjana
Sanjida
Sanna
Sansa
Santana
Santanna
Sanuthi
Sanvi
Sanya
Saoirse
Saphia
Saphina
Saphira
Saphire
Sapphira
Sapphire
Sapphire-Rose
Sara
Saraa
Sarah
Sarah-Jane
Sarai
Saraiya
Saran
Sarang

Saraya
Sarayah
Sare
Sareena
Sargun
Sariah
Sarina
Sarlota
Saron
Saroop
Sarrinah
Sarya
Sasha
Saskia
Satya
Sauda
Saule
Saumya
Savana
Savanah
Savanna
Savannah
Savannah-Leigh
Savannah-Mai
Savannah-Rae
Savannah-Rose
Savina
Savreen
Sawda
Sawdah
Sawyer
Saya
Sayeda
Sayuri
Sayyeda
Scarlet
Scarlet-Rose
Scarlett
Scarlette

Scarlette-Rose
Scarlett-Grace
Scarlett-Louise
Scarlett-Mae
Scarlett-Marie
Scarlett-May
Scarlett-Olivia
Scarlett-Rose
Scarlotte
Scout
Seana
Seanna
Sedef
Seema
Seerat
Sefora
Sehaj
Sehajpreet
Sehar
Sehej
Seher
Sehrish
Selen
Selena
Selene
Selihom
Selin
Selina
Selma
Sema
Sena
Senara
Senna
Sennen
Sera
Serafina
Serah
Seraphina
Seraphine

Seraya
Serayah
Sereen
Seren
Serena
Serenah
Serene
Serenity
Serenna
Seren-Rae
Seren-Rose
Serin
Serina
Serine
Serra
Seryn
Setareh
Setayesh
Seven
Shaam
Shaan
Shabnam
Shae
Shafa
Shah
Shahad
Shahana
Shahd
Shai
Shailene
Shaima
Shaina
Shaista
Shakira
Shakti
Shalen
Shalini
Shalom
Sham

Shama
Shamim
Shamiso
Shamiya
Shammah
Shana
Shanaaya
Shanade
Shanae
Shanai
Shanaiya
Shanay
Shanaya
Shanel
Shanela
Shanell
Shanelle
Shani
Shania
Shanice
Shanika
Shaniya
Shaniyah
Shannon
Shantel
Shanvi
Shanya
Shanza
Shanzay
Shara
Sharanya
Shareen
Shari
Sharifah
Sharleez
Sharlene
Sharna
Sharni
Sharon

Shauna	Shola	Sienna-Rose
Shawna	Shona	Siera
Shay	Shoshana	Sierra
Shaya	Shravya	Sierra-Mae
Shayana	Shreena	Siham
Shaye	Shreeya	Sila
Shayla	Shreya	Silva
Shaylee	Shrishti	Silvana
Shayleigh	Shriya	Silver
Shayma	Shukri	Silvia
Shayna	Shya	Silvie
Shaza	Shyanne	Sima
Shazia	Shyla	Simar
Shea	Shylah	Simarpreet
Sheema	Sia	Simay
Sheikh	Siaana	Simi
Sheila	Sian	Simisola
Sheindy	Siana	Simona
Shekinah	Sianna	Simone
Shelbie	Sianne	Simra
Shelby	Siara	Simrah
Shelley	Sibeal	Simran
Shelly	Sibel	Simranpreet
Shereen	Sibella	Simrat
Sheridan	Sicily	Simreet
Sheza	Sidney	Simrit
Shi	Sidonie	Sinai
Shianne	Sidra	Sinead
Shifa	Sidrah	Siobhan
Shifaa	Siena	Siona
Shifra	Sienna	Sira
Shiloh	Sienna-Grace	Sirat
Shira	Sienna-Leigh	Sireen
Shireen	Sienna-Louise	Siri
Shirin	Sienna-Mae	Sirin
Shirley	Sienna-Mai	Sirine
Shivani	Sienna-Marie	Siwan
Shiying	Sienna-May	Siya
Shiza	Sienna-Rae	Siyana

Siyona
Skaiste
Skarlet
Sky
Skye
Skyela
Skye-Louise
Skye-Marie
Skye-Rose
Skyla
Skyla-Grace
Skylah
Skylah-Mae
Skylah-Rose
Skyla-Leigh
Skyla-Mae
Skyla-Mai
Skyla-May
Skylar
Skyla-Rae
Skylar-Leigh
Skylar-Louise
Skylar-Mae
Skylar-Mai
Skylar-May
Skyla-Rose
Skylar-Rae
Skylar-Rose
Skyler
Skyler-Ann
Skyler-Rose
Skylyn
Sloane
Sloka
Smilte
Sneha
Snow
Soffia
Sofi

Sofia
Sofia-Grace
Sofiah
Sofia-Mae
Sofia-Marie
Sofia-Rose
Sofiat
Sofie
Sofija
Sofiya
Sofiyah
Sofiyya
Sofya
Soha
Solana
Solange
Soliana
Solomia
Somaya
Sona
Sonali
Sonam
Sonia
Sonya
Sookie
Sophea
Sophia
Sophia-Grace
Sophia-Jade
Sophia-Leigh
Sophia-Mae
Sophia-Mai
Sophia-Marie
Sophia-May
Sophia-Rose
Sophie
Sophie-Ann
Sophie-Anne
Sophie-Grace

Sophie-Louise
Sophie-Mae
Sophie-Marie
Sophie-May
Sophie-Rose
Sophy
Sora
Soraiya
Soraya
Sorayah
Sorcha
Soriah
Soriyah
Sorrel
Sotiria
Soumaya
Soumya
Sreeya
Sri
Srishti
Stacey
Stacie
Stacy
Star
Starla
Starlet
Starr
Stefani
Stefania
Stela
Stella
Stephanie
Stevie
Stevie-May
Stina
Storm
Stuti
Su
Suaad

Suad
Subhana
Sude
Sue
Sufia
Suha
Suhaila
Suhana
Suhani
Suhavi
Suhayla
Sukaina
Sukayna
Sukhmani
Sukhpreet
Suki
Sukie
Sultan
Sumaira
Sumaiya
Sumaiyah
Sumaya
Sumayah
Sumayya
Sumayyah
Sumeya
Sumeyye
Summaya
Summayah
Summayyah
Summer
Summer-Grace
Summer-Lea
Summer-Leigh
Summer-Lilly
Summer-Louise
Summer-Mae
Summer-Mai
Summer-May

Summer-Rae
Summer-Rose
Summer-Willow
Sunaina
Sundus
Sunnie
Sunny
Sunshine
Supriya
Sura
Surabhi
Suraiya
Suraya
Surayya
Suri
Suria
Surina
Suriya
Suriyah
Surraya
Surya
Susan
Susana
Susanna
Susannah
Susanne
Susie
Suzana
Suzanna
Suzannah
Suzanne
Suzi
Suzie
Suzy
Svana
Svea
Swara
Sybil
Sydnee

Sydney
Sydney-Rae
Sydney-Rose
Sydnie
Syeda
Sylvia
Sylvie
Syna

20
NAMES BEGINNING WITH T

Taaliah
Tabasum
Tabatha
Tabita
Tabitha
Tahani
Tahiba
Tahira
Tahiya
Tahlia
Tahreem
Taia
Taiba
Taibah
Taijah
Taisia
Taiya
Taja
Tal
Tala
Talah
Taleah
Taleen
Tali
Talia
Taliah
Taliah-Rose
Talia-Rose
Talitha
Taliya
Taliyah
Tallis

Tallula
Tallulah
Tallulah-Belle
Tallulah-Rae
Tallulah-Rose
Talula
Talulah
Talullah
Talya
Tamana
Tamanna
Tamar
Tamara
Tamarah
Tamera
Tamia
Tamiah
Tamilore
Tamira
Tamiya
Tammy
Tamsin
Tamsyn
Tamzin
Tamzyn
Tanae
Tanatswa
Tanaya
Tanayah
Tania
Tanisha
Tanishka

Tanith
Tanitoluwa
Taniya
Tansi
Tansy
Tanvee
Tanvi
Tanwen
Tanya
Tanzeela
Tanzila
Taqwa
Tara
Taraji
Taran
Taranpreet
Taraoluwa
Tarlia
Taryn
Tasfia
Tasfiyah
Tashi
Tasmia
Tasmin
Tasmiyah
Tasneem
Tasnia
Tasnim
Tasnimah
Tate
Tatenda
Tatiana

Tatianna	Teegan	Thelma
Tatum	Teela	Theodora
Tatyana	Tegan	Theresa
Tavia	Tegen	Therese
Tavneet	Tehilla	Theya
Tawana	Tehreem	Thia
Tawny	Tehya	Thiya
Taya	Tehzeeb	Thomasina
Tayah	Teifi	Thora
Tayana	Teigan	Thuraya
Tayba	Teja	Tia
Taybah	Teleri	Tiah
Tayibah	Temilade	Tia-Leigh
Tayla	Temilola	Tia-Louise
Taylah	Temiloluwa	Tia-Mae
Tayla-Mae	Temitope	Tia-May
Tayla-Rose	Temperance	Tiana
Taylor	Teniola	Tianah
Taylor-Grace	Teodora	Tiana-Rose
Taylor-Louise	Teresa	Tianna
Taylor-Mae	Tereza	Tiannah
Taylor-Mai	Teri	Tianna-Rose
Taylor-May	Terri	Tianne
Taylor-Rae	Tesni	Tiara
Taylor-Rose	Tess	Tia-Rae
Taymiyyah	Tessa	Tiaraoluwa
Tayyaba	Tessie	Tiarna
Tayyiba	Testimony	Tiarni
Tayyibah	Texas	Tia-Rose
Tazmeen	Teya	Tibyan
Tazmin	Thais	Tiegan
Tea	Thalia	Tierney
Teagan	Thandeka	Tiffany
Teah	Thandiwe	Tiffany-Rose
Teal	Thea	Tiger
Teala	Theadora	Tiger-Lilly
Teddi	Thea-Grace	Tigerlily
Teddie	Thea-Rose	Tiger-Lily
Teddy	Theia	Tiger-Rose

Tiggy
Tilda
Tilia
Tillie
Tillie-Mae
Tillie-Mai
Tillie-Rose
Tilly
Tilly-Anne
Tilly-Lou
Tilly-Louise
Tilly-Mae
Tilly-Mai
Tilly-May
Tilly-Rose
Timea
Timeea
Tina
Tinashe
Tinaye
Tippi
Tirion
Tirzah
Tisha
Tiwatope
Tiya
Tiyana
Toba
Toby
Tola
Tolani
Toleen
Toluwalase
Toluwalope
Toni
Toni-Leigh
Tooba
Tora
Tori

Torie
Tori-Leigh
Tova
Toyah
Tracy
Treasure
Tricia
Trinity
Trinity-Rose
Trisha
Trixie
Trudi
Trudie
Trudy
Tsering
Tsion
Tuana
Tuba
Tugba
Tula
Tulin
Tulip
Tulisa
Tulisha
Tullulah
Tulsi
Tululah
Tuppence
Twyla
Tyanna
Tyla
Tyler
Tyra
Tziporah
Tzivia

21
NAMES BEGINNING WITH U

Ugne
Ugochi
Ula
Uma
Umaima
Umaimah
Umaira
Umairah
Umaiza
Umama
Umamah
Umarah
Umaya
Umayma
Umaymah
Umaynah
Umayrah
Umayyah
Ummayah
Ummayyah
Umme
Umme-Habiba
Umm-E-Hani
Umrah
Una
Unaisah
Unaysah
Ursula
Urszula
Urte
Urwa
Urwah

Uswa
Uzma

22
NAMES BEGINNING WITH V

Vaani
Vada
Vainavi
Vaishnavi
Valencia
Valentina
Valentine
Valeria
Valerie
Valerija
Vanesa
Vanessa
Vani
Vania
Vanisha
Vanshi
Vanshika
Vanya
Varnika
Vasiliki
Veda
Vedika
Veera
Vega
Venice
Venisha
Venus
Vera
Verena
Verity
Veronica

Veronika
Vesper
Vesta
Vicky
Victoire
Victoria
Victory
Vida
Vidhi
Vidya
Vienna
Viha
Vihana
Vikasni
Viktoria
Viktorija
Vilte
Vimbainashe
Vina
Vinisha
Viola
Violet
Violeta
Violet-Mae
Violet-Rose
Violett
Violetta
Violette
Virginia
Vita
Vitoria

Vittoria
Viva
Vivian
Viviana
Vivien
Vivienne
Viya
Viyan
Vlera
Vogue
Vrinda

23
NAMES BEGINNING WITH W

Wafa
Wafaa
Wajeeha
Wajiha
Wan
Wanda
Wania
Waniya
Warda
Wareesha
Warisha
Weaam
Wen
Wendy
Weronika
Whitney
Wiam
Wiktoria
Wilhelmina
Willa
Willow
Willow-Grace
Willow-Mae
Willow-May
Willow-Rae
Willow-Rose
Wilma
Winifred
Winnie
Winny
Winona

Winter
Winter-Rose
Wren
Wynter
Wynter-Rose

24
NAMES BEGINNING WITH X

Xanthe
Xara
Xena
Xenia
Xi
Xin
Xinyi
Xyla

25
NAMES BEGINNING WITH Y

Yael
Yagmur
Yakira
Yalda
Yaminah
Yana
Yara
Yaren
Yasemin
Yashfa
Yashika
Yashna
Yashvi
Yasmeen
Yasmin
Yasmina
Yasmine
Yasna
Yasra
Yaz
Yazmin
Yehudis
Yelena
Yi
Ying
Yitty
Yixin
Ylva
Yoana
Yocheved
Yohana

Yohanna
Yolanda
Yosan
Yousra
Ysabella
Ysabelle
Ysella
Yu
Yuhan
Yui
Yulia
Yumna
Yuna
Yusra
Yusraa
Yusrah
Yussra
Yuxi
Yvaine
Yvette
Yvie
Yvonne

26
NAMES BEGINNING WITH Z

Zaara
Zaarah
Zadie
Zafiah
Zafreen
Zahara
Zaheen
Zahira
Zahirah
Zahra
Zahraa
Zahrah
Zaiba
Zaima
Zain
Zaina
Zainab
Zainah
Zaineb
Zainub
Zaira
Zairah
Zakirah
Zakiyah
Zala
Zamzam
Zaneta
Zaniah
Zaniyah
Zanna
Zara

Zarah
Zara-Maria
Zareen
Zareena
Zareenah
Zaria
Zariah
Zarina
Zarish
Zariya
Zariyah
Zarwa
Zaya
Zayah
Zayba
Zayna
Zaynab
Zaynah
Zeena
Zeenat
Zeenia
Zehna
Zehra
Zeina
Zeinab
Zelah
Zelal
Zelda
Zemirah
Zena
Zenab

Zendaya
Zenia
Zenna
Zenobia
Zerya
Zeynab
Zeyneb
Zeynep
Zhara
Zhi
Zi
Zia
Ziana
Zianne
Zienna
Zikora
Zikra
Zilan
Zimal
Zina
Zinnia
Zion
Zirwa
Zissy
Zita
Ziva
Zivah
Zixin
Ziya
Zlata
Zoe

Zoey
Zoeya
Zofia
Zoha
Zohal
Zohra
Zoja
Zola
Zora
Zosha
Zosia
Zoya
Zoyah
Zsofia
Zubaida
Zuha
Zuhra
Zulaikha
Zulaykha
Zulekha
Zuleyha
Zumra
Zunaira
Zunairah
Zuri
Zuriel
Zuza
Zuzana
Zuzanna
Zuzia
Zyana
Zyla
Zynah
Zyra
Zyva

BABY GIRL NAMES

JAMES AND ROSE HUGHES

HAS THIS BOOK HELPED YOU?

If this book has helped you narrow down your choice of a baby name then feel free to head to Amazon and leave us a review.

We'd be really grateful!

Printed in Great Britain
by Amazon